Language, learning and remedial teaching

Explorations in Language Study
General Editors
Peter Doughty   Geoffrey Thornton

LANGUAGE, LEARNING AND REMEDIAL TEACHING

Roger Gurney

EDWARD ARNOLD

© Roger Gurney 1976

First published 1976
by Edward Arnold (Publishers) Ltd
25 Hill Street, London W1X 8LL

ISBN 0 7131 0081 8

Explorations in Language Study

Language in the Junior School
E. Ashworth

Language and Community
P. S. and E. A. Doughty

Language Study, the Teacher and the Learner
P. S. Doughty and G. M. Thornton

Language, Brain and Interactive Processes
R. S. Gurney

Explorations in the Functions of Language
M. A. K. Halliday

Learning How to Mean: Explorations in the Development of Language
M. A. K. Halliday

English as a Second and Foreign Language
B. Harrison

They Don't Speak Our Language
(Ed.) S. Rogers

Language in Bilingual Communities
D. Sharp

Language, Experience and School
G. M. Thornton

Accent, Dialect and the School
P. Trudgill

Printed in Great Britain by Butler & Tanner Ltd
Frome and London

General Introduction

In the course of our efforts to develop a linguistic focus for work in English language, which was published as *Language in Use*, we came to realize the extent of the growing interest in what we would call a linguistic approach to language. Lecturers in Colleges and Departments of Education see the relevance of such an approach in the education of teachers. Many teachers in schools and in colleges of Further Education recognize that 'Educational failure is primarily *linguistic* failure', and are turning to Linguistic Science for some kind of exploration and practical guidance. Many of those now exploring the problems of relationships, community or society, from a sociological or psychological point of view wish to make use of a linguistic approach to the language in so far as it is relevant to these problems.

We were conscious of the wide divergence between the aims of the linguist, primarily interested in describing language as a system for organizing 'meanings', and the needs of those who now wanted to gain access to the insights that resulted from that interest. In particular, we were aware of the wide gap that separated the literature of academic Linguistics from the majority of those who wished to find out what Linguistic Science might have to say about language and the use of language.

Out of this experience emerged our own view of that much-used term, 'Language Study', developed initially in the chapters of *Exploring Language*, and now given expression in this series. Language Study is not a subject, but a process, which is why the series is called *Explorations in Language Study*. Each exploration is focused upon a meeting point between the insights of Linguistic Science, often in conjunction with other social sciences, and the linguistic questions raised by the study of a particular aspect of individual behaviour or human society.

5

The volumes in the series have a particular relevance to the role of language in teaching and learning. The editors intend that they should make a basic contribution to the literature of Language Study, doing justice equally to the findings of the academic disciplines involved and the practical needs of those who now want to take a linguistic view of their own particular problems of language and the use of language.

Peter Doughty
Geoffrey Thornton

Contents

Introduction

In my own book in this series, *Language, Experience and School*, I claimed that little serious attempt had yet been made to evolve, in the remedial departments of our secondary schools, teaching techniques based upon 'sound linguistic principles'. In this book, Roger Gurney takes us a long way towards remedying this omission.

He begins, in a first chapter pointedly entitled 'Why remedial?', by subjecting the notions underlying the whole concept of remedial education to critical examination, and follows this, in his next chapter, 'Who is remedial?', by asking what kinds of pupil are most likely to find themselves in remedial groups. He looks closely at the criteria which are traditionally used to label pupils as remedial, and suggests that what we now know about the nature and function of language makes these criteria no longer adequate.

Chapters 3 and 4 are devoted to an account of our present understanding of the language-learning process. The central insight here is the concept of *language as meaning*, especially as developed by M. A. K. Halliday in his book in this series, *Learning how to mean*. Roger Gurney's account makes clear the extent and complexity of the child's accomplishment when he acquires the foundations of his language early, very early, in his life, and, thus, the scope of the linguistic resource that the child brings with him into school as the basis of his whole learning effort.

The first important thing that schools do for their pupils is to teach them to read and write, and the next three chapters discuss some of the linguistic considerations that must be taken into account if pupils are to be enabled to invest their linguistic resource most profitably in the accomplishment of this task. This discussion focuses on various aspects of the relationship of sound to symbol that links speech to its written representation. Here understanding is vitally necessary to those whose job it is to teach pupils entering secondary schools with a mastery of the writing system insufficient to enable them to perform the learning tasks with which they will be confronted.

Roger Gurney then reconsiders the part that assessment of progress should properly play in the process by which these slower pupils learn to read and write adequately, before coming, in his final chapter, to the implications for classroom practice of what he has been arguing at a theoretical level. The title of the chapter, 'Meaning, Method and Materials', summarises his approach. Language is for making meaning. Therefore, if a pupil is to be enabled to use language in the classroom, and thereby improve his mastery of it, he must be put into a position in which he can make meaning with language. This demands a method of working on the part of the teacher that will make this sort of learning situation possible, and the use of materials designed to help the pupil realize the desired objective. Roger Gurney here brings theoretical considerations into relationship with what goes on in classrooms where remedial pupils are being taught.

The book, as a whole, constitutes a powerful plea for relevant insights to be focused, through the teacher, upon the problems of the pupil in so-called remedial teaching. It calls for a clear-headed analysis of those problems, and the devising of teaching strategies thought capable, in the light of present linguistic knowledge, of enabling pupils to solve them. Like all the books in this series, its main concern is to promote a greater awareness and understanding of the role of language in individual development and learning, although its concentration is upon the problems of those who, for some reason or other, find certain aspects of learning difficult. It should prove invaluable to remedial teachers—and their pupils.

Geoffrey Thornton

1 Why 'remedial'?

'In Nature there's no blemish but the mind;
None shall be called Deformed but the unkind.'
Antonio in *Twelfth Night*

1. Introduction

The term 'remedial' reflects a concern about the educational
attainments of a proportion of children in the school population.
It implies that a remedy is needed to get these children's work
to a satisfactory level. This quasi-medical analogy may be taken
even further, because a diagnosis of the problem must be a pre-
condition for effective intervention. For instance, a child's reading
ability may be poor. On analysis, various of the contributory skills
of reading are found to be particularly deficient and therefore
likely causes of difficulty. Alternatively, if the problem is
numeracy, then equivalent deficiencies in number concepts and
processes are pinpointed. Suitable activities, materials, books and
programmes of work are then prescribed to effect the necessary
change.

But here we must pause for thought, to consider whether our
medical analogy is entirely suitable. Like many technical words,
the meaning of 'remedial' has been influenced by the circumstances of its use. When we use phrases such as 'remedial education', 'remedial children' or 'remedial classes', we are using the
word 'remedial' in a sense different from the one it bears under
other circumstances. A remedy is usually taken to be some action
or substance which restores a previous, and better, state of affairs.
But, whatever the difficulties, there is really no question of
remedial help applying to the diminution of skills which were previously satisfactory and are not now. In other words, loss of skill

11

is not a criterion for a child to get remedial help. More often than not the skills under consideration have never been satisfactory, and so one is dealing with a problem of lack of development, not the restoration of faculties previously acquired. Remedial help, in brief, is founded upon the notion that, for some children, certain abilities need to be developed so that they may catch up with their peers.

2. The roots of concern

Those abilities upon which attention is focused are the basic educational attainments, such as reading, spelling, handwriting and mathematics. Very rarely does anything other than problems with literacy, numeracy and certain behaviour difficulties, cause as much concern. But there are other abilities which are important for individual development; the skill to handle interpersonal relationships, for instance. Seldom do schools see lack of progress in this sphere as warranting remedial attention, yet it parallels the other difficulties in involving demands on a child's linguistic abilities.

The reason for the literacy/numeracy emphasis is not hard to find. A school's purse strings are in the hands of men and women who are accountable to the nation's tax and rate-payers. It is their duty to allocate money so that society will reap the most benefit. It is also the case that their decisions will be affected by, and reflect, society's attitudes towards those in need. This is particularly so where the provision is seen as a direct link to society's needs.

Industrialized countries, such as ours, are quick to recognize the importance of literacy as one of the cogs which keep the wheels of the economy turning. The same can be said of numeracy. The prospect of an illiterate or semi-literate working force is seen in terms of economic catastrophe. The consequences would seem so dire that money and facilities are more readily available to finance and support remedial services—as long as these are directed towards literacy/numeracy. In brief, then, we are prepared to put money into helping with reading difficulties because there are powerful educational and economic reasons for doing so. This is part of a political attitude towards children which sees them, in the mass, as economic potential, an investment in the future. The emphasis on literacy in the school curriculum is consistent with the view that equates standard of reading with standard of employability. Putting this in a slightly less abrasive way, we can say that financial limitations are the reason why greater and more general help is not available for other difficulties.

In theory, there is no reason why the 'remedial' label should not be attached to any group or service where children are being helped to catch up, though there seems to be something inherently absurd about the idea of 'remedial art' or 'remedial music'. In practice, 'remedial' nearly always implies help with the 3 Rs and often help with only 1 R, Reading. The reason why other aspects of the curriculum do not command such attention is that they do not have the same socio-economic value as literacy and numeracy. The emphasis on these problems, therefore, is as much a politico-economic affair as it is an educational one.

3. The needs of the individual

Though help is concentrated on what would seem to bring most benefit to society, this also corresponds to what we consider important for the development of each individual. As adults, we may not feel that lack of musical ability, say, is any great handicap in everyday affairs, but lack of reading ability is almost certainly felt as a social stigma. People will go to incredible lengths to avoid showing they cannot read, yet be quite happy to admit they haven't any idea what is under a car bonnet or how to fix an electric plug. On another level, a poor degree of literacy must be a severe limitation in finding suitable employment. Besides this, however, there is the question of the personal satisfaction which comes from being able to share fully in the literate society in which we live.

4. The implementation of help

Given the fact that remedial help is limited to certain educational abilities and no others, our next consideration must be that this help is often implemented in a most inefficient and haphazard fashion. I shall confine myself to a brief outline of these limitations, however, as they represent policies which are only marginally within the influence of teachers in general. More important by far are the strategies of help that a teacher may implement for him- or herself. It remains a cruel paradox that, despite the emphasis on helping to solve their problems, it is the weaker remedial children who are sacrificed in the struggle for educational survival, as a result of decisions made within school by responsible teachers and headteachers.

Quite patently there is considerable variation from area to area and from school to school in the provisions for remedial help. Some authorities seem to ignore the problem altogether. Even where facilities do exist, teachers may have to work under quite inadequate conditions with few resources.

It is a matter of great concern that very few teachers have had more than a smattering of training in remedial techniques. Such is the result of a lack of courses at university and college level. The situation, in this regard, is getting better but there is still too much of a do-it-yourself attitude about much remedial training. Not that this situation applies only in remedial education. It is, in fact, part of a more widespread problem which relates to reading and teacher training generally. Many teachers in primary schools have to learn about reading and reading development on the spot because they have had little or no training in such matters at college. All these difficulties are serious impediments to effective remedial help.

My principal concern in this book, however, is with analyses and programmes of work which remedial and class-teachers can use themselves with a minimum of external help. Effective help must depend on good teaching allied to relevant diagnostic techniques. The point is taken that these abilities are best fostered in a systematic fashion through professional courses.

5. What price literacy?

If we accept that there is a desperate need to help some children to greater proficiency in academic skills, particularly in literacy where some effort is being made, then there are still other problems to consider.

The provision of remedial facilities is something of a two-edged sword as far as the children themselves are concerned. On the one hand, they desperately need to be the same as other children, yet the only means of attaining this end is by being treated differently. They have to go into the limbo of the remedial group before they have a hope of emerging into the salvation of mainstream education. All too often they are put in a state of suspended educational animation, condemned to a diet of reading primers, reading skills and inconsequential writing exercises until they can prove, by dint of improved reading ages, that they are fit to be taught by the more usual educational methods.

This would not be so bad if they all had a good chance of emerging again quickly, but this is not so. Progress is often slow and a child may remain in the remedial group until he leaves school. To see how this may come about, even with well-intentioned help, we have to look at the circumstances and conditions which these children face.

In the first place there is the morale and expectation of the participants to consider. We use the phrase 'remedial children' as if, in some sense, they needed help to become 'proper children'. From this start it is very easy for a teacher to slip into the habit of thinking of them as intellectual cripples. To talk of 'children with reading problems' may be long-winded but it is more accurate and, in the long term, fairer.

One of the great problems for these children, it would seem, is the difficulty they have in establishing themselves as learners. After all, they are brought together because of their failures. The emphasis on what they can't do, on what they haven't achieved, leads, not unnaturally, to expectation of further difficulties and failure. There is a fair amount of research which suggests that the children will not disappoint us in this respect. They will accommodate to our expectation of them by producing what we indicate they are capable of doing.

The establishment of different methods to teach fast and slow reading groups is one way of translating differential expectation of ability into reality. In one first-year class that was studied, the slow group was subjected to very deliberate formal teaching, with little in the way of relaxed informal talk to accompany it. By contrast, the same teacher dealt with the fast group in a completely different manner. They were taught, as a group, in a very relaxed atmosphere. They were allowed to talk freely and became much more animated as a result.

It is also the case that, where a teacher suspects children of being of lower ability, he or she is likely to teach them less (4). It seems, then, as if teachers react to the seriousness of actual or imminent reading difficulties by becoming more solemn themselves and by limiting what they undertake. Not only does this create a situation in which learning is joyless, but the grimness and formality are likely to inhibit learning through undermining a child's confidence. He will reason—'If teacher is worried about my reading then things must be very serious.'

It must be very difficult for a teacher to remain optimistic and cheerful in the conditions under which many have to work. Their charges are the ones who most need experienced teachers, stability, lack of distraction and good surroundings. In practice, it is not uncommon for the remedial group to be working in the corridor, the cloakroom, the medical room or the hall. It is the remedial group which is most likely to be found wandering round the school in search of a temporary home. It is the remedial group which is disbanded because their teacher is covering the absence of a class teacher. It is the remedial group which is often taken by part-time teachers with little experience. Even in schools with large permanent remedial departments it is the young inexperienced teachers who end up with the remedial stream. Such a state of affairs is disheartening for both the children and the staff concerned.

The influence of the school in creating the conditions of continuing failure may be even more subtle. In an article entitled 'How teachers learn to help children fail', Estelle Fuchs is concerned with the theory that it is the slum-school's belief in the social conditions outside the school creating the high failure rate which makes those failures inevitable. She shows, through the experience of one young teacher, how the other school teachers create such a belief over the course of the young teacher's first year of teaching. The result is that:

'the slum-school gradually instills, in even the best-intentioned teacher, the rationale for its own failure: the idea that it is the slum, it is the child and the family who fail, but never the school'. (23)

These are some of the difficulties and dangers of creating groups based on comparative failure in reading. But what is the answer? To leave a child floundering, without any additional help, is surely criminal. Far too many schools do adopt this attitude, justifying their ostrich-like posture with remarks about 'not having any serious problems in the school' or 'this is all one could expect from these children anyway'. The alternative may not be to set up remedial provisions in a half-hearted manner either. This is likely to do as much harm as good. Where remedial departments are created, they should have good facilities, well-trained staff and the confident backing of the rest of the staff. The constant undermining of the position of remedial teachers is one of the worst features of our present educational system.

A part of the answer must be to cope with problems more effectively within the normal classroom. This will take the pressure off the other, more specialized, facilities. Such an idea is not really an alternative to remedial help, as both are within the compass of most schools.

6. Conclusion

It is my hope that this book may be of some use both to the specialist remedial teacher and to those teachers who have to deal with learning problems within the normal classroom. A point that I hope will emerge strongly is that remedial does not imply grossly different. Neither the teaching methods nor the children concerned have any characteristics inherently different from those found in the usual classroom. Good remedial methods are simply good teaching methods, and what is practised in remedial groups or classes need not be confined to those situations. The capable remedial teacher looks for the level at which a child is competent in order to work forward from there. This means that the activities and methods used are often equivalent to those employed with younger children who are progressing satisfactorily. A two-way flow of information and ideas on teaching methods between the remedial and the ordinary class teacher is needed. In the final analysis both are concerned with the same problem—getting children to read efficiently.

These perspectives take on a new significance when we come to discuss language and the remedial child. I intend to show how the emergence of a linguistic perspective to educational difficulties has added both a powerful new dimension to our analyses and a framework for tackling many problems. The significance of this work for the rest of education is that the insights and methods gleaned in the remedial field are almost certainly applicable elsewhere too.

2 Who is 'remedial'?

'In truth most definitions of illiteracy amount to this—"that he is illiterate who is not as literate as someone else thinks he ought to be".'

Ministry of Education. *Reading Ability Pamphlet 18*

1. Children in remedial groups

It is natural to inquire what kind of children one may find in remedial groups. Who are they? What needs remedying? What characteristics do they have? What haven't they got? These questions are related and it is difficult to separate them completely. In the sections that follow the interlocking of these problems will become more apparent.

2. Who are they?

First we need to make a distinction between 'Who is remedial?' and 'Who gets remedial help?' In the previous chapter I made the point that remedial help has social implications, since it is limited to the basic educational attainments which are considered the *sine qua non* of the economically useful man. If we were to use 'remedial' to apply to anyone who had not developed their attainments to a satisfactory level then there would be few, if any, who escape this net. I count myself as extremely wanting in most practical subjects, for instance. On this basis the answer to 'Who is remedial?' is 'I am—and I suspect everybody else must be too.'

If we now turn to 'Who gets remedial help?' we find that two kinds of answer are involved. The first is that anyone with severe difficulties in reading, writing, spelling and number is a candidate for help. This immediately begs the question of 'How severe is severe?' and 'How do you assess this, anyway?'. These are questions to which I shall return later in the chapter.

A second kind of answer relates to the provision of remedial help discussed previously. The countrywide variations that are to be found mean that children who qualify for help in one area would not do so in another. Even within one authority it may depend on which school a child attends whether that child gets remedial help or not.

3. What characteristics do they have?

The policy associated with most remedial help is to group children together on the basis of some common characteristic, usually that of reading difficulties. At first blush this would seem to imply similar difficulties associated with the reading problem. However, this is not so; reading difficulties, for instance, fall into any number of different categories and the children within one group may all have different problems. The same applies to other difficulties too. The remedial group, in fact, may consist of children with visual problems, auditory problems, the slower learner, the child with speech difficulties and so on. They all need different help, and a factor to consider here is the variation in help available from area to area. This, in turn, is related to local conditions such as population density, local industry, housing conditions and so on. The children in different remedial groups vary considerably in the severity and types of difficulty which they show. For instance, the children in an inner-ring school who are largely immigrant have very different problems from the children at school in the affluent suburbs.

4. What haven't they got?

It may be the case that the remedial, like the poor, are always with us. This is no reflection on present or future educational systems; it relates to a statistical fact. Half of any population are, and will be, below average for a particular skill. It doesn't matter whether this refers to reading, writing, fishing or computer programming. It doesn't depend on the average level of skill in the population. Where differences exist they divide any group, in effect, into the 'haves' and the 'have-nots'. For example, we may take some highly select groups such as airline pilots, cabinet ministers or kings of England and assess them on their abilities. No matter that few people could aspire to such positions; we may

19

still apply the epithets 'good' or 'bad', 'inspired' or 'indifferent', on the basis of whether they have or haven't carried out their duties as we would like.

This fact points up a further problem: are we concerned with absolute or relative difficulties? Are we concerned about the level of a skill or about the individual's standing relative to others? The answer is, and must be, that both aspects are important. We must be concerned about the level of a skill where it relates to job demands and individual aspirations. We must be concerned about an individual's relative standing where it affects his sense of his own worth and other's expectations of him. Both aspects, in fact, are already criteria for remedial help and their use tends to confuse the issue of identifying characteristics even further.

Returning to this question of characteristics, it might be thought possible to equate 'have-not' with remedial, but this is not possible. In the first place we are concerned not just with below average performances, but with those that are significantly below average. This leaves room for discussion, since we then have to agree on what constitutes significance. In the second place, as mentioned previously, it makes a considerable difference to one's chances of help what skill is considered deficient. The 'have-not' of one skill is not necessarily the 'have-not' of another and one cannot, therefore, use one to estimate the other. But how often, as teachers, do we fall into the trap of underestimating what a child can do because he is a poor reader, say? Besides this, only a few skills are considered worthy of remedial interest, curriculum-wise. The 'have-nots' of PE, music and religious knowledge do not attract the same educational attention.

The question, then, of whether a 'have-not' is considered to be a remedial problem is not one to be decided solely on the characteristics and performance of the individual concerned. We have to determine what skill is below par and whether it is sufficiently poor to warrant attention. The matter, it appears, turns on the value of certain skills in society and on the values of current educational thinking. We look to see whether the problem is literacy or numeracy and whether the child is significantly behind his peers in this respect. If both of these conditions are fulfilled he is likely to receive extra attention.

Put like this we see that a description of remedial education and remedial children should include, simultaneously, both the characteristics of a group of children and the characteristics of conventional educational practice. It is impossible to separate one from the other, just as it is impossible to characterize the whole group of remedial children in terms of what they lack.

The implication must be that in attempting to help others we, as teachers, must look at ourselves, what we are doing and why we are doing it. In other words, what we are doing must be set within the context of a coherent theory of language and learning that involves both teacher and pupil. This double focus is an essential ingredient of all we should be doing in remedial education; it is a cornerstone of this book.

5. What needs remedying: the problem of assessment

The question of 'What needs remedying?' cannot be separated from the further question of 'Who is in need of help?'. In other words, it is not sufficient to say that children need remedial help because their reading is poor and leave it at that. We must specify, for each individual, what they find difficult and how they may be helped. It is specially important for these children to recognize the individuality of their abilities and needs. To minimize this fact, by treating all remedial children as one uniform problem, is to do them a disservice.

(a) Who needs help?

While the emphasis is on reading difficulties, what is said in this section is equally applicable to other educational attainments. But, whatever the difficulty, the first problem for a teacher is whether to undertake, or ask for, an assessment of a child at all. Is additional help needed? In one sense the teacher has got to assume that something is wrong before undertaking such a step. There is usually the feeling that the child ought to be doing better than he is. What the teacher sees, in other words, is that, had circumstances been different, the child could have attained a satisfactory level of attainment. There is surely no point in undertaking an assessment, for remedial purposes, of a child who is achieving what one expects of him. Or is there?

The question of absolute or relative levels of reading has already been raised. Are we concerned about a child's present reading level or about his performance relative to others? Asher Cashdan gives the following answer:

'the important issue is not the normative one—how children compare with each other or with the average for a particular age—

but rather the effective level of literacy they eventually reach'. (12)

There can be few who would disagree with such sentiments. However, for the teacher trying to make a decision about a child with reading difficulties, it begs the question. What exactly is the effective reading level that the child is going to reach? The answer is, lamentably, that we don't know. Despite the thousands of experimental studies of reading and its difficulties, we do not have the data to make reasonable predictions about the long-term growth of individual reading abilities. If we had, it would be much easier to say whether a child actually needs additional help or not.

The fact that we can't make accurate predictions about future reading ability has forced teachers and psychologists to look at alternative methods of assessing whether help is needed. In practice, this has meant some sort of comparison with other children or other abilities. Here we come to the idea of unused potential. If a child's abilities in other respects are found to be satisfactory, yet reading is not, then it has been the practice to assume that the child has unused potential, as far as reading is concerned.

The comparison of one child with another is a very rough method of assessing future reading levels. By picking out those children who are relatively poor at reading, one is inferring that they are the potential illiterates or semiliterates. Traditionally these terms have been used as follows:

> Reading age between 7–9 year level—semi-literate
> Reading age below 7 year level—illiterate

A reading age of 7 years, for instance, is the level of reading one would expect from an average 7 year old. Of course, if one finds a child with such a reading level it is not an automatic qualification for remedial help. One wants to know what the child's actual age is. If he is 10 years old then there's a problem; if he is 6 then he is doing better than average.

There are a number of criteria for picking out those children, the 'backward' readers, that are significantly behind in their reading. The first is to select a particular discrepancy, greater than two years, say, between reading age and actual (chronological) age. The difficulty with this is that the older the child, the less significant the discrepancy becomes. A reading age of 10 at 12 years is not as bad as a reading age of 6 at 8 years old. This problem is overcome, to an extent, through using the same data to produce a Reading Quotient. The formula for deriving this figure is as follows:

$$\text{Reading Quotient} = \frac{\text{Reading Age}}{\text{Chronological Age}} \times 100$$

It has been usual to take Reading Quotients below 80 as delineating the backward reader.

The trouble with such an approach to reading difficulties is that it picks out the needy in an approximate way without indicating possible causes of difficulty or the potentiality for changing the situation. Because of the limited availability of resources for remedial help, there is always this problem of giving help where it will be most effective.

The dilemma for our teacher is only partly resolved. He or she can say that a child is over 2 years behind in his reading or that his Reading Quotient is less than 80 and that, therefore, somebody should take a closer look at him. But what of children who don't fall conveniently into this category? What is to be done about them? Should one ask for help? These are unresolved questions and, perhaps, formulate the problem in the wrong way. The teacher is probably asking him- or herself what she can do to help. The answer to this is—'quite a lot'. What sets the limit to this help are the practical difficulties of finding time to do so and the theoretical problems posed by the lack of adequate formulations of learning difficulties.

(b) What is wrong?
At this point I want to discuss some of the concepts that are, and have been, used in carrying out a fuller examination of reading difficulties.

Historically, one of the first ideas to emerge was that reading did not match up to other abilities, particularly intellectual ones. The French psychologist Binet provided detailed evidence of what abilities could be expected within the school population at given ages. From this data it was possible to compute a mental age for the intelligence of the child. In effect, what Binet's test allowed one to say was, 'This child, who is x years old, has a performance on the test which is comparable to that of an average child y years old.' This concept of ability, evquivalent to the developmental level of an idealized average child, was the fundamental

23

idea behind 'mental age'. It enabled the assessor to sort out the retarded children from those who were just backward in their reading. Backwardness, in this sense, meant any discrepancy between actual age and reading age. Within this backward group there would be the sub-group of children supposedly working below their mental ages. Take, for instance, a child of 10 years with a mental age of 9 years and a reading age of 8 years. He would be considered backward in reading by two years, though only one year retarded. No retardation was attributed where mental age and reading age were the same.

The retarded child became the focus of attention because it could be demonstrated that he had unused potential. The assessment of his general intellectual abilities as being higher than his reading attainment was taken to mean that he would be a better candidate for help. This kind of approach was very influential for some time and then lost a lot of its appeal when Binet's original concept of mental age was abandoned. It became clear that there were statistical and psychological objections to its use and, therefore, to the implementation of policy resting upon it. It is extremely questionable, for instance, whether children of the same computed mental age but of differing ages actually have the same intellectual abilities. Despite these objections many people still act as though the concept were tenable.

Of course, no one is going to deny that intelligence plays a part in the development of reading abilities. However, it is only one of many factors that have been isolated. At present we do not know how it combines with other abilities to give the basis for the one, overall activity. Intelligence is certainly involved in reading, but not in any simple relationship which is easy to demonstrate. The use of the mental age statistic in equating intellectual ability with reading ability is very dubious practice. In fact, this is dubious practice no matter what is involved. The fundamental hypothesis in remedial teaching is usually that there is some discrepancy between what the child is and could be achieving. We then look for reasons why this should be so. It is very easy to pick on some wayward function and assume it is the cause of the problem. But, unless one can show what is happening, it is not justifiable to promote the association to a cause and effect relationship. Even if it is, one cannot tell in which direction it is operating. In fact the discrepancy hypothesis itself must be suspect, because of the implicit reliance on normative data.

In any case we are not concerned, as Asher Cashdan said, with how a child compares with others, but with what reading level he will eventually reach. Until we know what the patterns of reading development are, we have little guide about future performance from present abilities. Because a child is below average at present does not mean that this will obtain in the future. Even if it were so, the actual level of the future ability is what should concern us.

As an aside, I would suggest that a major source of difficulty for the remedial services stems from the use of inappropriate measures and the kind of outdated ideas which have been instanced above. Many of these, though not all, are perpetuated within the ordinary schools and classrooms themselves. It is essential, therefore, that both the class teacher and the remedial teacher know what ideas are current, what abandoned, and what the strengths and weaknesses of present measures are. This is particularly important since fresh concepts are continually emerging in the replacement of previous ideas. For instance, children's abilities tend to be measured in terms of very specific skills and functions nowadays. There is much less emphasis on determining an overall Intelligence Quotient. The preferred statistic in most of the present tests is one which compares a child's performance against the rest of his age group. His score is a measure of where he stands within, or how much he deviates from, the norm of that group.

Many of the present psychology tests consist of a battery of sub-tests which sample the sub-skills of what is being tested. The well known and much used Wechsler Intelligence Scale for Children is a good example. When this is combined with other tests it yields a profile of an individual child's strengths and weaknesses on a variety of skills and sub-skills. This enables a psychologist to pinpoint gross difficulties in relation to the poor educational attainments. The idea behind such an approach is that these particular difficulties are, and have been, the limiting factors to progress. Remedial help may then be directed towards improving the child's 'specific learning difficulties (disabilities)' as they have been called.

The apparent usefulness of this approach should not blind us to the theoretical difficulties it leaves in its wake. One American worker (16) believes that the concept has lost a lot of its usefulness through being spread over too many definitions and approaches. Besides this, however, there are other limitations. First of all, it is obvious that the discrepancy hypothesis is still a major feature of the present approach. That is to say there is an assumption that the cause of the problem lies in those skills or abilities which are found or assumed to be below average. The deviation scores of the sub-tests represent comparisons with a standard. Without this implied comparison the basis for remedial action is lost. As one psychologist has put it, 'The result of your analysis is to show that the child is exactly where you would expect him to be.'

The intrinsic difficulty with many of these theories of learning disabilities is that they pre-empt alternative explanations by turning what is an hypothesis into a statement of fact, viz. that poor academic attainments are the result of deviant abilities in specific skills and processes. Hence:

'Children who have learning disorders are those who manifest an educationally significant discrepancy between their estimated intellectual potential and the actual level of performance related to basic disorders in the learning processes . . .' (1)

and

'A child with learning disabilities is one with significant intra-developmental discrepancies in central-motor, central-perceptual, or central-cognitive processes which lead to failure in behaviour reactions in language, reading, writing, spelling, arithmetic and/or content subjects.' (36)

The circularity of both definitions is patent. They are concerned to say that learning disorders (disabilities) are seen as educational discrepancies which result from some inferred difficulty with basic (central) processes. In other words, a learning disorder relates to a cultural expectation of average attainment. If a child does not achieve this, then there must be something basically wrong with his learning processes.

Is it small wonder, then, that Chalfant and Scheffelin complain—'At this point in time, we probably know more about learning failure than we do about the learning process itself.' (14). One is left wondering how relevant this information is to the need for effective help. It seems that we need theories of how children learn under varying circumstances and not simply how they fail.

6. Misgivings

To an impartial outsider the assessment of a child with learning difficulties must appear to be a very one-sided issue. This is because too many people in education assume that the purpose of the assessment is to see what is 'wrong' with the child, with a view to putting it 'right'. The emphasis, in other words, is upon

26

the child's inadequacies in relation to the educational difficulties. We look at how they fail and not how they succeed. The implication being that, if we can determine the likely causes of failure, we can then put them right by some course of action aimed at the areas of weakness.

But is this fair? After all, the child's difficulties occur in a given educational context in the presence of one or more teachers. What is the influence of this context on the child's performance? Obviously the teachers and the school have an effect upon the child but we are not often made aware of this in discussing individual problems. A recent article by Patrick Meredith puts this kind of criticism of the system very pungently. He writes:

'Hell-bent on conforming to the ethics of an education system geared at all levels to Thorndike's concept of "getting ahead of somebody", generations of educational psychologists have been reared on a diet of psychometrics whose function is to demonstrate degrees of ineducability, to assign educational failure unequivocally to defects in the child, in his home, in his parents and in his heredity, and never to failures of teaching, failures in school organisation, failures in urban conditions, failures in commercial ethics, or failures in educational legislation.' (42)

As an example of this attitude we may quote part of Eisenberg's definition of specific reading disability. It reads: 'We are concerned with the children who *fail to learn to read*, despite *adequate classroom instruction. . . .*' (19). Here, within the space of one sentence, we have the exoneration of the teacher and teaching methods coupled with the indictment of the child for failing to learn. Need more be said?

7. Summary

We have to face the fact that there has been no adequate formulation of learning difficulties to provide an unambiguous description of the problems and an acceptable rationale for solving them. Perhaps no one such theory could exist. What is obvious is that we are unlikely to find out if we continue to use the present tactics. The circularity of the learning disability definitions leads to confusion about what is cause, what result. What we need is empirical evidence unclouded by definitional bias. All we have at the moment are hypotheses about why children fail to match our expectation of them. Until we can demonstrate how the discrepant abilities are causally related to low attainments the concept of specific learning difficulties, for instance, must remain an hypothesis. What we need, in fact, are theories of learning and not of failure to learn. It means looking at the same data as at present, but in a different conceptual framework. The difference may be subtle but it is crucial to those we are trying to help. We must give these children their self-respect, by treating them positively as learners. Only in this kind of an atmosphere, which does not reinforce notions of failure, can we hope to provide effective help for those children who need it.

3   Home and school

'I used to think I was poor. Then they told me I wasn't poor,
I was needy. Then they told me it was self-defeating to think of
myself as needy, I was deprived. Then they told me deprived was
a bad image, I was underprivileged. Then they told me under-
privileged was over-used, I was disadvantaged. I still don't have
a dime. But I have a great vocabulary.'

Caption to a Feiffer cartoon

1. The sociological perspective

During the 1950s and 1960s new ideas gave an entirely different
emphasis to a lot of work concerning language and the low academic attainments of certain children. In particular, two important influences emerged bearing upon child development and language. Both were taken up by psychologists with some fervour.

The first was Chomsky's work on transformational grammar.
His theories had no direct bearing upon learning difficulties, but
they did lead to a study of children's language in its own right
and not just as a poor version of adult abilities. This trend was
a significant pointer to later developments. At the time, however,
it was simply part of the general excitement over what has been
called 'the rediscovery of children's language'.

Language became the focus of attention for another reason too.
It promised to provide the crucial link between early learning at
home and later learning at school. This second trend, developed
initially in America and of a much more practical nature, was
concerned with the low-level attainments of certain groups of
children, particularly Negro, poor and working-class ones (or
combinations of these attributes). It was noted, by comparison
with white, rich, middle-class children, that they tended to have

fewer toys, books or any of those material possessions which seem, intuitively, to provide the early learning basis for schools to use later for academic purposes. In short, the home circumstances seemed to be relatively impoverished, with the further implication that these children would be at a disadvantage in the educational system compared with the more favoured middle-class children.

On both sides of the Atlantic there was a good deal of investigation into the possible causes of the low academic attainments of these groups. In this country the research undertaken for the Plowden Committee and by others (18, 60) had shown that, for the primary school children in these studies, the home and neighbourhood effects were apparently much greater than those of the school in influencing academic attainments. Since poverty and lower-class status were both closely associated with low attainments the spotlight had fallen, not unnaturally, on the contrasted way of life between poor and rich, between working-class (often lower working-class) and middle-class. In particular, it was felt that children brought up in such environments were missing out materially, linguistically and culturally. Terms such as 'under-privileged', 'linguistically deprived', 'culturally deprived' were coined to denote what the environment, and the home in particular, were not supplying. As a consequence, projects, programmes and charities were organized to provide part, at least, of what the parents were unable to supply in the early years of a child's life. The emphasis was largely on the language aspects since it seemed that this was the key to the problem. A typical statement is to be found in the Newsom report:

'The evidence of research suggests that linguistic inadequacy, disadvantages in social and physical background, and poor attainments in school, are closely associated. Because the forms of speech which are all they ever require for daily use in their homes and in the neighbourhoods in which they live are restricted, some boys and girls may never acquire the basic means of learning and their intellectual potential is therefore masked.' (48)

The one particular theme of such theories related to the discrepancy between middle-class and working-class children on verbal tests. Since the working-class group scored lower, on average, here was direct proof of fundamental difficulties which would affect schooling. But what was the cause of this verbal deficit? An obvious solution seemed to be that these verbal attainments were a direct reflection of language abilities. Further, that these child-
30

ren were not able to achieve as much at school because of lack of language as a mediator between their abilities and their performance. Since language developed at home initially, particularly through the mother–child interaction, here was the obvious source of the child's later difficulties at school.

These ideas gained further impetus from the research and theory which Bernstein was developing in England through the early 1960s and onwards. His was the same concern as those holding to the verbal deficit theory but based on differential social learning and attitudes rather than psychological comparison. Bernstein proposed the existence of two codes, 'restricted' and 'elaborated', relating to language behaviour. The restricted code was particularly associated with the speech characteristics of lower working-class children. Its implication for the child's formal education were this:

'In the learning of this linguistic form the child is progressively oriented to a relatively low level of conceptualisation. It induces a lack of interest in processes, a preference to be aroused by, and to respond to, that which is given immediately, rather than responding to the implication of a matrix of relationships. In turn, this will affect what is to be learned and how it is learned and so influence future learning.' (5)

Many took Bernstein to mean, or to imply, that the language of working-class children was an inferior tool for educational purposes. If their language could be improved it would mean that teachers would have a much easier time in developing the children's attainments. Bernstein was to refute their assumptions later (6) but, by then, the idea of inferior working-class language had become very firmly rooted in the folk-lore of educational thinking.

This sociological option to the question of learning difficulties appeared as an alternative to the psychological one. Basically it followed the same line of reasoning, but indicting the home or the culture for not providing the child with adequate learning 'tools'. In these formulations it was the home or the culture which was deviant for not supplying the right language or experience for the developing children. Such terms as 'language deprivation' (blaming the mother) and 'cultural deprivation' (blaming the culture or sub-culture) were current. Although it is not immediately apparent, such notions are based on normative data too. As Baratz and Baratz (2) point out, the standard for the comparisons is the white middle-class. Particularly in America and, to a

31

lesser extent in Britain, vast programmes have been mounted under the rubric of 'compensatory education'. Their driving impulse has been to supply the missing incredients which would put the 'deprived' children on a firm educational footing.

There are two points to note here. The first is that sociological ideas about the important influences in education have evolved at a rapid rate. The quotation at the head of this chapter is an apt comment on the transitory nature of the sociological labels. The succession of such labels, to indicate impoverished conditions, is a reflection of changing theoretical attitudes and dissatisfaction with previous formulations. The second point is part of this evolution of ideas. There is now increasing unease about the use of normative data in relation to the comparison of different social groups. If we assume, for a moment, that the comparison is valid, then we must admit it is a very inefficient method of helping those in need. If one is going to work on group statistics then many, in the group that receives help, will not need it. The converse is also true. In any case, there would be many who would question the theoretical basis to such comparisons. They would argue that the differences they highlight bear little relationship to what is known about the groups in sociological terms.

2. Comparative studies and the concept of 'potential'

The two research themes of the previous section differed in their theoretical backgrounds. Broadly, the first was linguistic and the second sociological. Besides this, however, there was another less noticeable, though significant, difference. The psycholinguistic studies were much less concerned with the behaviour of one set of children in relation to others. In these, language was being studied for itself, not as an inferior or superior variety, but as a topic in its own right. Admittedly the children's language, was by implication, a developing adult form. Still the change represented a dramatic alteration in approach to language development.

The other sets of studies, based on the verbal deficit theory, drew their theoretical formulations from the different attainments of the groups they compared. This constituted a version of the norm-oriented approach mentioned in previous chapters. It involved an implicit assumption of unrealized potential. The group with the lower attainments is seen as capable of matching the superior one, given different circumstances. It amounts to saying 'The middle-class can do it. Why can't you?'

There are two points to be made here. Firstly, there can be no doubt that academic attainments represent, in some way, the fulfilment of children's potential. Secondly, on a statistical basis, it is reasonable to expect two large groups to be fairly similar in average attainment. The difficulty arises when one tries to formulate hypotheses using the two propositions in combination. For instance, the significant social group differences that are to be found have been interpreted as if they are a functional deficit on the part of the working-class group. Similarly, differences in the attainments of one individual have been taken as a psychological indication of unused potential.

I would suggest that the interpretation of the sociological or psychological data in terms of either 'underfunctioning' or of 'unused potential' is unwarranted. If these objections are sustainable, then they must raise the whole question of educational programmes based upon such questionable premises. If the premises are questionable, then it would be prudent to re-examine the programmes and what they are seeking to achieve.

First of all let us examine the argument that, if a child's attainments do not match his other abilities or those of others, then he is failing or underfunctioning. We can say that the development of particular skills and abilities to particular levels means that a child's original potential is being realized in very specific ways; only a few of the innumerable developmental options are taken up. If, as an adult, you become a school teacher then it is unlikely that you are also realizing your potential to be an accountant, a car mechanic, a shop assistant or prime minister at the same time. You may, though, be a good parent, an average car driver, a poor gardener and so on, thus 'failing' to take up your options to have reached some other level in those behaviours. Each individual has, at any given moment, a limited number of achievements and abilities and, at the same time, has an infinite number of states which are not displayed. If this is failure, then we all fail. A more serious objection is that it leads to ridiculous conclusions. For instance, by being a good reader one is failing to be an average or poor reader at the same time. This must surely be nonsense. It only makes sense to talk of potential being realized positively, in particular ways; it can have no negative value. Similarly, it must be nonsense to suppose that the good driver must be the good gardener and the good reader and so on. There may be a reasonable statistical probability of this being so, but there is no 'must' or 'ought' about it. To put a descriptive value on below-average attainments stems from implicit social attitudes concerning 'normal' behaviour and not from psychological theory.

What can one say, then, of the related, but more neutral, position which maintains that the difference in attainments between classes, or between intelligence and attainments in one individual, is a demonstration of 'unused' potential? It seems to be a very weak scientific stance, since there is no way of verifying or denying such a statement. Potential must refer to the sum-total of possible future states and behaviours and not to present attainments. The latter can only be referred to a child's potential at some previous time. This argument, that concurrent attainments and abilities may be matched for potential, is fraught with many theoretical difficulties.

In fact, the concept of unrealized potential harks back to the old 'bottle filling' ideas of education. The child was seen as an empty vessel to be filled up through education. In this analogy, unrealized potential would be equivalent to not filling the bottle fully. But such ideas are far too simple and mechanistic since they ignore the developmental, interactional nature of educational progress. It is permissible to say 'At time T_1 this child had these potential behaviours which, at time T_2, were realized by set A actual behaviours,' but not, 'This child with set A behaviours has failed to develop sets B, C, D, E and so on.'

Similarly, a child or a group of children cannot 'under-function'; they can only function. One can say 'At this moment I would predict for reading, say, that $R - R_n$ is the range of reading attainments that the child could display at time T in the future.' There is little point in saying 'This child, displaying attainment R_{10}, is underfunctioning because there were higher values in his potential set of attainments at some previous time.' One could say equally well that the child is overfunctioning in respect of other values in the set. This, in fact, was one of the difficulties in the use of the mental-age concept.

Both the 'underfunctioning' and the 'unrealized potential' concepts have social values built into them by implication. They say to the child, in effect, 'You had the potential to do this and you are underfunctioning because you have not realized that potential. You ought to have done so. We will investigate to find out what went wrong (and to apportion the blame).' This attitude is based on a view of life which sees every person as capable of conforming to the norms of society. To err in either direction is

34

likely to bring suspicion and censure, because to do so implies the deliberate adoption of deviant behaviour. Of course, such views work on a very restricted concept of potential. They should be looked at in this light and judged accordingly.

It should be made clear at this point that to question the assumptions behind much remedial work is not to question the need for the help itself. That is another matter altogether. There is obviously tremendous scope for further aid, based on sound teaching principles. Even if no remedial children existed, there would still be a very good case to be made for improving the help we extend to the learner reader. But we do know that undoubted class and individual differences exist both in educational attainments and verbal skills. Both may be significant pointers to the need for remedial help. What is being argued is that it is not reasonable to base the help on these differences nor on the notion of inadequate language. The help must be based on the way individuals actually learn.

3. Specific criticisms

I now turn to some of the criticisms which have been directed at the language-deficit theories. For instance, Horner and Gussow (35) have demonstrated that, in studies of the language of lower-class children, the focus has been on the forms of speech and not on how language functions. This emphasis, which reflected what was then the current interest in grammar, gave a perfectly valid description of language but was a dubious prescription for effective help. They point out that the detailed formal analysis tended to imply the uncovering of 'trouble spots', together with an approach to eliminate or modify such problems, resulting in enhanced learning abilities. In other words, help is based on deviations from an implied norm. The parallel with the 'specific learning difficulty' approach in psychological analysis is quite marked, as the reader may have noticed. The two approaches share another common feature: a lack of explicit supporting evidence for their formulations.

Horner and Gussow have criticized the language-deficit approach, saying that it has not provided evidence for its contentions. They have called for a change in approach so that we view language from a functional standpoint. They say that the importance of language to education is in what it does and not what it consists of. This is a call to which Halliday's work seems an adequate response, as we shall see in the next chapter.

He himself had pointed out earlier (29) some of the difficulties of measuring children's language objectively. If one measures vocabulary or grammar alone then the result may be a very misleading indicator of language ability or development. The reason is that these two structural aspects of language are inseparable parts of learning how to mean. At times both aspects may be developing together but, at others, one may develop on its own. To measure one alone, then, cannot be a reliable guide to linguistic ability.

Over and above this argument, however, is a further problem of what one is trying to measure and whether it is possible to do so. Halliday poses the question of how an investigator is to overcome the difficulties raised by considering both the quantity and the quality of a child's language. He concludes: '. . . there is no reliable way of saying "this child has a smaller linguistic inventory (than that one, or some presumed standard)"'; and it would not help us much if we could.'

4. Present trends

I have attempted to show how a concern over children's academic attainments became a concern about their language abilities as well, and how approaches to the problem are limited through the bias of their formulations. In particular, the emphasis upon structure to the detriment of process leads to a situation where meaning and the interactive processes of learning are given less attention than they might. The concern with verbal deficit and its emphasis upon comparison with the standards of others leads to notions of failure, culpability and retribution in the form of certain types of 'compensatory' education. It is perhaps not too far-fetched to see the Bereiter and Engelmann programmes as a form of punishment!

One of the most disquieting features about this latter trend has been the almost universal practice of absolving schools and the existing educational provisions from their part in determining the level of the academic attainments of 'disadvantaged' children. As Bernstein noted (6) it is silly to talk of compensatory education when the children concerned have not had the benefit of 'an adequate educational environment' in the first place.

At the present time, however, there has been a radical shift in the theoretical positions of the studies being undertaken. The realization that some important things had been missed from earlier studies has led to an increasing concern with the content of child speech as well as its form (53). Slobin reports that there is a growing awareness of the child as an active participant in its own acquisition of language. This has meant a much closer linking of theories of linguistic and intellectual development, for instance. The outcome has been to focus on the child as a learner, processing information by means of linguistic and other strategies. This will be the subject of the next chapter.

4   The child as learner

'Thus the important terms are those that are salient to the child rather than to the adult observer.'

Kessen

1. Introduction

A current emphasis in many areas of research is the investigation of the child as an active participant in its own cognitive development. This applies both to intellectual and linguistic matters. The child is viewed as a positive processor of information, active on its own behalf, but limited by its own state of knowledge and development. For instance, Bever (8) has shown that children's comprehension of speech depends on the strategies they employ to decipher it. The way that a given utterance is segmented to extract meaning changes with time, as cognitive abilities change.

This research trend represents a theoretical stance which, if carried through to all educational practice, would undoubtedly vindicate its positive approach. Particularly where remedial help is concerned, the emphasis upon the child as learner (in contrast to being a failure) has much to recommend it. In this light let us take a brief look at one or two investigations to see what they can tell us about early learning, in general, and the basis for reading, in particular. Later, we are going to have to look at the reading process from these vantage points. We can look at reading both as a linguistic-cum-intellectual activity and as a medium for employing information processing strategies. First, however, we must take a look at what is known about the early general development of such systems.

2. Language and thought

The precise relationship between language and thought has

always been a controversial issue and, in practice, some of the most influential theories concerning these cognitive processes have tended to emphasize one at the expense of the other. Theorists concerned with linguistic development have pointed to the fact that intelligence has little effect on the timing of language acquisition (39). In contradistinction Piaget, for instance, has always maintained that intellectual operations are the principal processes of cognitive development. Language is merely an aid to advancing these abilities.

The present position seems to be that there is a much greater influence of one process upon the other, in the early stages of development, than had previously been supposed. If such ideas are sustainable, and they seem to be, then there is going to be a lot of rethinking about the implications for early schooling.

3. Early language and learning; 'nature's' strategy

Even if we adopt the older view of the two behaviours developing separately, there is a remarkable similarity between them in the young child. During the first year of life the young baby moves from an early period of dependency and reflex behaviour through to a later stage of increasing independence and voluntary, exploratory movement. During this period as well it becomes possible for the trained observer to differentiate clearly what we regard as intelligent behaviour and speech.

While it is usual to talk in terms of the beginnings of a child's intelligence even from the very early weeks of life, there is not anything clearly recognizable as language behaviour until the second half of the first year. It was Piaget who demonstrated that the child's early physical behaviour is a manifestation of intellectual powers. It also forms the basis for later development where thought processes are construed as internalized actions or operations. The functional beginnings of our intellectual abilities lie in the experience and behaviour of the first year of life. Further, it is the internalization of these observable behaviours which account for the development of that abstract ability we call intelligence. On the other hand the production of speech, indicative of language abilities, does not appear from the outset. What does is, initially, reflex sound and, later, random babbling. Neither activity displays the hallmark of language but, nonetheless, they are its precursor, a kind of protolanguage. The development of a whole range of vocal sounds, with clear and consistent discrimination between them, is a condition for the child to be able to display that other abstract ability we call language. Both language and intelligence rely on early motor abilities and herein lies the source of their similarities.

The table below charts the comparison over the first 18 months of life:

VOCAL ACTIVITIES

(0–1½ m.) Early vocalization such as birth cries are reflex. These gradually become more differentiated and distinct.

(1½–6 m.) In the first phase of babbling the child becomes aware of the sounds it is making. The tongue is used in an experimental way to produce gurgles and coos. The child is playing with sound.

(6–9 m.) The child begins to repeat sounds it hears in the second phase of babbling. He begins to respond to the sound of his own voice to produce lalling, the repetition of the same sound or syllable e.g. dadadada. . . .

(9–18 m.) The third phase of babbling begins with the imitation of sounds that others make, echolalia. During this period the child seems finally to 'get the idea' of what language is about. There is a shift towards using only those sounds required of the mature language user. At some point the first word is produced.

(18+ m.) The two-word stage is reached and the internal language organization of grammar becomes apparent. As Halliday has said: 'Grammar makes it possible to mean more than one thing at a time.' (30)

SENSORI-MOTOR ACTIVITIES

(0–1 m.) Early movements such as sucking are reflex in character. They become more efficient as time progresses.

(1–4 m.) This second stage consists of primary circular reactions in which simple acts are repeated for their own sake.

(4–6 m.) In the third stage (secondary circular reactions) the child repeats acts that are interesting to him e.g. kicking.

(6–10 m.) The child begins to coordinate secondary reactions in this fourth stage. Simple problems are solved and the responses are used to obtain a desired goal e.g. moving one object to find another.

(10–18 m.) Tertiary circular reactions characterize this fifth stage. The child conducts trial and error experiments, varying the response in order to obtain the desired goal.

(18+ m.) At this point the internal intellectual organization of problem solving is much in evidence. As Piaget has said of this sixth stage: it is characterized by 'invention of new means through internal mental combinations'. (49)

Nature's strategy, to put it anthropomorphically, is to set the scene and to leave the child to take it on from there. The spontaneous, and reflex, production of physical movements and vocalizations produce interesting environmental events which catch the interest and attention of the child. In the case of movements he can observe and hear the results of that movement. Gradually, the child comes to establish a connection between the two. By his own efforts, that is, he develops intellectually. Similarly, his own spontaneous vocalization will produce interesting environmental events in the form of his mother's attention and her verbal responses. Gradually, one imagines, the idea dawns that he can use his vocal powers deliberately to control these gratifying results. At this point, surely, the basis for future linguistic development has been laid? Once vocalizations are used for this conscious function the child has it within its powers to work out a system of communicating his wishes to others. At the same time he starts the process of deciphering the messages others are communicating to him. Eventually the two aspects merge when he develops the ability to encode his messages in a more public form of communication. At this point he can abandon the very personalized protolanguage, that individual system he has concocted for himself.

Piaget's account of the further development of the higher intellectual functions are well known through his own writing and the interpretation of others. They will not be elaborated here. The reader is referred to Piaget (50), Piaget and Inhelder (51), and Beard (3) for introductory accounts of his work.

What has not been available, until comparatively recently, has been an account of linguistic development on a functional basis. This has now been supplied by Halliday. The reader should consult *Learning How to Mean* in this series for the full acount. (31)

4. The functions of language

Halliday has developed his model of language learning from the detailed study of one child, Nigel. In this he follows Piaget's early exploratory studies of child development which were limited to Piaget's own children. Because of the limited nature of the evidence it is fair to say that the findings must be taken as provisional until further studies confirm the general outlines. Halliday has said, however, that each child may, at times, follow quite idiosyncratic paths through the phases of language development. Thus further studies are likely to map common pathways and to supply fresh evidence of the individuality which a child brings to the process of learning.

Three developmental phases became apparent in this analysis: an initial functional system (Phase 1), a transitional system (Phase 2) and the learning of the adult system (Phase 3). Here we will be concerned with just the first two phases, leaving the discussion of the adult system and abilities to the next chapter.

Phase 1 The emphasis on function in this study means that we have here a theoretical connection with the general cognitive development which appeared during the babbling phase of the first few months of life. At the point Halliday starts his account of Nigel's linguistic development at 10 months, Nigel is using his vocalization for four distinct language uses or functions. Up to this time Nigel's use of sound had not been consistent enough to warrant a 'linguistic' label. At 10 months this changed and it was possible to designate sounds unambiguously as functionally significant, since they were used on a considerable number of occasions with readily identifiable meaning.

The consequence of adopting this functional approach is that language behaviours are apparent before words appear. There is just sound and meaning, no structure. In this, too, Halliday's account differs from previous descriptions of language development which have taken the first word as the starting point of language. Here the child is seen to develop his own individual sound-meaning connections for specific purposes long before words appear.

From the beginning four generalized functions are present in Nigel's linguistic system. These are:

Instrumental	—'I want' function
Regulatory	—'Do as I tell you' function
Interactional	—'Me and you' function
Personal	—'Here I come' function

The first two are severely practical uses of language and the second two relate the individual to his personal/social environment. All must, in some degree, relate to other cognitive development. For instance, the separation of the self from the non-self, which Piaget describes, is an obvious prerequisite, for all these functions incorporate the self into language. They all have an element of 'I' about them. Despite this fact, each language function is completely distinct and autonomous. There is no overlap.

Phase 2 At about 16 months of age Nigel moved into the very brief second phase. This appears to be transitional between the initial system of single sound-meaning connections and the adult system in which one utterance will contain a number of meanings simul-

42

taneously; a change from meaning one thing at a time (using one function) to meaning many things at a time. The change is accomplished through the introduction of structure, such as lexis and grammar, into the child's linguistic system.

At the start of this phase the first words are used and a rapid development of vocabulary follows. This, together with the introduction of grammar, means the child is now able to engage in dialogue. Admittedly most of his conversational vocabulary is limited to observation and recall, but this will finally extend to prediction as well.

Three further functions are added to the linguistic repertoire before Phase 3 begins. The next two to develop, the Heuristic and the Imaginative, appear to be related:

> Heuristic —'Tell me why' function
> Imaginative—'Let's pretend' function

The first allows the child to explore the environment through language, the second allows the child to create its own imaginative environment through linguistic play.

Later in the phase the Informative function develops as well:

> Informative—'I've got something to tell you'
> (which you didn't know before) function

The use of language for the deliberate conveyance of information is a tremendous step forward in cognitive development for it heralds the incorporation of social concepts into the linguistic system. Up to this point the child's participation in conversation has depended on the promptings of others. Before, Nigel could not initiate dialogue, though he could use his language functions to answer questions, greetings, calls and so on. Now he can initiate it and this means he has internalized the social concepts of speaker and listener in order to take part in conversation.

The rapid development of vocabulary is part of the extension of existing functions through the setting up of structure within the system. Besides this, it plays a part in opening up new abilities such as dialogue. Occasionally, now, two functions are combined in (and through) the use of one word. In particular, there is a development associated with learning about the environment personally. Previously the separation of the self from the non-self had allowed the Personal and Heuristic functions to develop. Now these combine to give a more elaborate learning function which enables the child to categorize what he observes in terms of words

43

which are already formulated within the culture. In other words, he is extending his own interests by learning what words adults use for particular phenomena.

In Nigel's case, the lexical explosion was quickly followed by the structural-grammatical one in which word strings were used on one intonational pattern to give the first structured utterances. At this point Nigel started, too, to use intonation in a systematic way to denote the major functional distinction of this phase, between learning through language and the other practical uses. Halliday refers to these more general differences and functions as the mathetic (learning) and the pragmatic (the rest of the original functions) macrofunctions.

What is clear about Phase 2 is that it paves the way for Phase 3. The incorporation of vocabulary, grammar and intonation into the linguistic system extends the range and flexibility of what the child can do with its utterances. At the end of this phase, through grammar and dialogue, the child has some grasp of the adult language system, which it will continue to learn and exploit for the rest of its life. It has accomplished this feat largely through its own efforts, through using sound to develop its purposes and meanings.

5. Language strategies

Children's speech is a reflection not only of developing linguistic functions but also of developing cognitive processes. In a study of children's speech Katherine Nelson (47) uncovered a number of interesting facts which complement Halliday's work. The emphasis of her study was semantic-intellectual rather than semantic-linguistic. Nelson's research aimed to uncover the in-tellectual categorization of the child's world as reflected in its speech. She was concerned with phase 2 and onwards.

On page 45 is the general key to the semantic of the world that the child comes to develop. It is based on intuitions about the child's use of situational and context rules, though the categories within the key were usually self-evident, according to Nelson:

The children's vocabulary was analysed on a 'parts of speech' basis, once a 50-word level had been reached. All the different categories of the key were present from the beginning, with general nominals predominating. Two groups of children were distinguished on the percentage of their general nouns in their

44

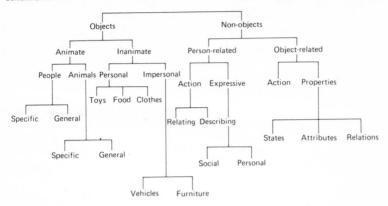

vocabulary. The groups were designated Referential and Expressive:

Referential (largely general nouns—more than 50%)—object-orientated language

Expressive (person–social words and general nouns—less than 50%)—self-orientated language

It would seem quite possible to interpret these groups in terms of an emphasis on mathematic (the referential group) or pragmatic (expressive group) macrofunctions.

What is particularly interesting is that these different orientations have both cognitive and linguistic consequences. In terms of the general key, Nelson notes that all children first tend to fill in elements of all the major branches. This seems to correspond well to our notion of a child elaborating a number of language functions at this stage of development. From then on development, in terms of the key, could be either horizontal or vertical. The former reflects an emphasis that is shown as early syntactic competence, because of the potential it introduces for combining words into sequences. The latter, by contrast, reflects semantic development within particular domains of knowledge. Here syntactic development is limited by the lack of combinatorial potential. During this period the referential group's average utterance length was 2·4 words. By contrast, the expressive group's average was 12·6. This is one aspect of the contrast between the groups which results from the initial language differences.

The emphasis, by the referential group, on object vocabulary

45

has no early effect on the rate of acquisition of language. Later, though, this group tended to accelerate, giving rise to a very short, very rapid phase of lexical/structural development. (Nigel seems to have followed this pattern.) By contrast the language changes for the expressive group were continuous and gradual.

Nelson regards the expressive/referential dichotomy as an indication of different strategies in learning to talk. (Halliday also speaks of interactional and instrumental semantic strategies.) She says:

'The functional emphasis appears to affect both patterns of development and vocabulary at age 2 in addition to the content and form of the language acquired. The presumed underlying strategy is one of choosing different situations in which to talk and different objects and events to talk about . . .'

It seems that the child's strategies are relatively independent of the mother's linguistic influence. This lack of influence accorded to parental speech habits has been noted before (53). However, influences are apparent at particular times, and in particular ways. A high level of object naming is significant for a child's advanced linguistic development at 2 years but not at $2\frac{1}{2}$ years. Parental rejection of a child's stumbling attempts at words affects utterance length at 2 years and not later, and so on. These statistical effects, including those associated with the referential/ expressive dichotomy, tend to disappear in the later stages of development. The reason, it would seem, is that the nature of the developmental process changes and so do the environmental effects upon it.

Early on, the general pre-language cognitive hypotheses have a large effect upon the way vocabulary develops. Parental strategies of acceptance or rejection may help or hinder to a considerable extent at this stage. Later, with the development of the full linguistic system much of the earlier bias is lost. A full analysis reveals, however, that there are particular interactive effects relating to cognitive hypotheses, child strategies and parental feedback which are likely to have permanent consequences upon language development.

6. Comprehension and problem-solving strategies

I want now to pursue the subject of strategies a little further and to broaden the perspective somewhat. There are a number of points to make which are important for the overall theme of the book. These relate children's strategies to personality differences, stages of cognitive development and functional limitations.

(a) Personality differences play an important part in the choice of strategy. We have seen something of this in the previous section where the referential/expressive differences were mentioned. But, apart from this, the child has another important choice to make in making sense of the world around him; he has to decide whether to talk or listen in any situation. The talker can be seen as actively testing hypotheses and getting feedback from those around him, while the listener may not need to participate actively to get the information. A more deliberate form of the talking strategy is to ask questions. Early on, this tactic correlates well with vocabulary development.

Another strategy, which must have important consequences, relates to the child working on his problems after the event, as it were. Halliday cites an instance of Nigel returning to the theme of a particular conversation they had in Greenwich Park some hours before. It demonstrated how Nigel had adapted what had been said to his own functional capabilities. Clearly the incident had been exercising Nigel's mind in the meantime. It is a matter of the way he sees himself that he broaches the topic again. Evidently he sees himself as a person capable of working on a problem until it is solved.

(b) Strategies change with time as cognitive abilities change. In this connection Bever (8) has plotted the development of children's comprehension of speech through the strategies they employ. It seems that semantic clues are the dominant means of comprehending sentences, especially in mature language users. These signal the internal logical–grammatical relations, e.g. actor, action, object, modifier, through which utterances are segmented perceptually. The ability to assign such relations correctly develops with language experience but may have to depend on strategies with rather limited scope early on. For instance, in one strategy children assume that any noun–verb–noun sequence represents actor–action–object. A child who has not developed beyond this strategy cannot understand fully the passive construction which reverses this order. Complete comprehension has to await further cognitive development.

47

(c) In the third category we find that particular strategies may relate to functional limitations imposed by undeveloped abilities. These strategies, such as the comprehension ones mentioned above, are a means to an end. The classic studies of children's problem-solving undertaken by Vigotsky (59) may be quoted here. He showed that every time a young child of 4 to 5 years is confronted by a difficult problem, the child uses external speech to aid himself. His speech is directed towards himself and involves a statement of the situation, together with a description of those past experiences which the child thinks may help. In other words, the child is using speech as a strategy by which he may influence his own behaviour. Vigotsky showed that, in the initial stages, the child speaks aloud to himself and that, later, this speech is reduced to a whisper. Finally, at about 7 to 8 years of age, the child can solve complex problems entirely through internal speech, without the necessity for external aids.

Another commonly quoted limitation which calls for the deployment of strategies is short-term memory capacity. The amount of information that can be taken in at one time is limited and this, therefore, affects cognitive processes. However, the development of memory itself involves memory strategies and is therefore affected by other cognitive processes. John Hagen (28) particularly implicates rehearsal strategies in the development of memory span, i.e. repeating what one has heard. He has shown that both selective attention and verbal processes play a part in its development. He concludes that central memory increases with age, but only functions effectively in conditions which permit rehearsal.

As a final comment, we may turn to what Flavell (21) has said about development in the use of strategies. He points to two important types of developmental change: specific changes relating to, say, verbal rehearsal and general changes which involve planning on the child's part. The child becomes aware that if he undertakes some activity at this moment *then* he will improve his chances of success in the future. This latter point is very important for our discussion because it emphasizes the 'child as learner' theme. It is vital that the child should take active steps in learning through his own guidance and planning. This is a very potent way to make learning relevant and to increase the motivation of the child. The implication for education is, of course, that we must foster self-supportive skills.

5 Language, text and reading

'There are several aspects of learning to speak and learning to read that are common to many cognitive tasks.'

Frank Smith (54)

1. Introduction

In order to read effectively a child needs to be able to cope with several varieties of language, both oral and written ones. In fact, oral competence comes first, through the development and use of the initial language abilities. These oral abilities must be well advanced before a child can hope to get to grips with the complexities of the printed word.

The present chapter will explore some of these complexities and how the development of mature abilities becomes possible. Finally, we will discuss reading and how the differences between the written and spoken word create problems for the learner reader.

2. Adult conversation and its development

It has been traditional to speak of three major types of sentence function in utterances such as conversation. These types are statement, question, command and they relate, for example, to the work done in initiating the sequential parts of any conversation:

Part 1. A. What do you think of John? (Question)
       B. He's all right.
Part 2. A. I think he's fantastic. (Statement)
       B. Do you?
Part 3. A. But don't you dare tell him I said so. (Command)
       B. I won't, I promise.

In this short example of dialogue one person A controls the inter-action at each step. B plays her part by simply keeping the con-versational flow going, without attempting to alter its course. She acquiesces in allowing A the dominant, directive role.

Now, as adults, we all take for granted the ability to trade in such functions. In fact it is very difficult to imagine language with-out them and, correspondingly, it is very easy to assume that we have always been able to use statement, question and command forms. But this is far from the truth. A child has to learn these functions through the early speech interactions which were dis-cussed in the previous chapter. Let us, therefore, recap on this development and follow its course into the adult abilities of Phase 3, which Nigel reached at about 2 years of age.

In Phase 1 Nigel developed a number of separate language functions concerning his very personal needs. He had learned, among other things, to request goods or services, to express interest in objects or events and to acknowledge personal relationships. But he could only use one of these language resources at a time and could not cope with conversation. This was because he had no idea how to convey or request information by verbal means.

At the start of Phase 2, however, genuine dialogue appeared. Nigel made this possible by incorporating vocabulary and grammar into his language system. In other words, he started to verbalize in a way which would be understood by any competent speaker of English. As a consequence he also had to learn to cope with new social situations and interactions through this new lan-guage involvement. At first his abilities, in this respect, were rather limited since he could only take a role in conversation assigned by somebody else; he had no means of initiating conversation for himself. Nigel had yet to learn to think of himself as a source of information through language. He was to learn this through being asked simple questions. He learned about commands and state-ments, in a similar way, by verbalizing and repeating those he heard. He would be limited to a very passive role in conversation until he could master the types of sentence function associated with the manipulation of others. Through Phase 2 Nigel was work-ing towards such uses of language. Because of dialogue he was able to develop the distinct practical-personal functions of Phase 1 until he could cope with some of the complexities of mature lan-guage. At this point not only could he adjust his language to cope with the personal and social aspects of a conversation, but he could do both at once. This ability reflects the development of a more abstract language function (metafunction) which Halliday terms the Interpersonal metafunction.

Let us take a brief look at this system at the adult level to show how the competent speaker can select from a number of options in fulfilling his personal needs and wishes within a social framework. Starting from the question 'Are you free?' we may imagine four contrasting responses:

1. Yes, do you want some help?
2. What do you want now?
3. Yes, I am free, sir. Can I help you?
4. It depends what you mean by free, Mr. Brown.

The reader will be able to fill in quite a lot of the unspoken details concerning the circumstances, relationships and personalities involved in these snippets of conversation e.g.

1. A warm, informal relationship—though 'Are you free?' carries overtones of a business or professional association. The responder is giving the questioner an equal social footing.
2. A more aggressive response which could be construed as indicating either a strained relationship between social equals or else a more usual one between superior and subordinate.
3. This is a much more formal relationship which gives the strong impression of a shop assistant attending to a customer in a friendly businesslike manner.
4. The fourth response is also formal and indicates that, although couched in polite terms, the responder is not allowing the questioner much freedom to pursue his unstated purpose. The response can be construed as carrying a restrained hostility either to the person or to the implied demand.

These responses are summarized in diagrammatic form on the next page.

Looking back over the four responses we see that 'Are you free?' has been interpreted as 'Signal your readiness to do what I want.' It leaves the responder free to take whatever line or option he pleases. Contrast this with other alternative openings, such as 'Come and help me with this parcel, Peter' or 'Go and serve that customer, Mr. Jones' and it is apparent that the questioner has chosen a very undemanding option in introducing the topic of conversation.

Given such an opportunity to answer freely, the responder uses his language abilities to negotiate what he wants. He introduces his personal wishes by selecting a positive or negative response. Simultaneously, he takes up a social option which is realized, in

51

POSITIVE PERSONAL RESPONSE

INFORMAL RELATIONSHIP ← → FORMAL RELATIONSHIP

1. Yes, do you want some help?
(Personal friendliness)

2. What do you want now?
(Personal unfriendliness)

3. Yes, I am free, sir. Can I help you?
(Socialized friendliness)

4. It depends what you mean by free, Mr. Brown.
(Socialized unfriendliness)

NEGATIVE PERSONAL RESPONSE

part, by a scale of formality. Because his wishes have to be negotiated within a social framework, his language must be appropriate to the particular relationship. But, without the ability to exchange ideas, the personal-manipulative part of conversation would be impossible. This leads us to a consideration of how such abilities develop.

3. Information and learning

A most important aspect of Phase 2 concerned Nigel's use of language as a means to organize experience and categorize the world around him. Once dialogue emerged, the way was open to develop this aspect of knowledge and language, through tapping the resources of others, particularly parents. First, however, Nigel needed to think of people as sources of information. Then he could work at the linguistic means of obtaining it through his own questioning. But, initially, Nigel had to learn to think of himself as a source of information. This was accomplished through adults calling upon him to answer simple questions. His ability to respond, at this time, was limited both by a lack of realization of what communication was about and by the lack of means to express himself.

Gradually, Nigel learned to respond to a greater range of questions and to frame them himself. The major breakthrough occurred when he realized he could convey new information to a listener, not just what was already known and shared. His own Information function was thus developed and through it he was able to seek new information from others. Nigel started to ask questions of the 'What is that?' variety and in his own speech he distinguished intonationally between information that is already shared with the listener and that which is new. He gave to the latter an interrogative form.

We see here the mutual interaction of the developing aspects of language. Dialogue opens up social language interactions which, in turn, provide the means of developing information flow through language. Question and statement types provide the means for accomplishing this and they, in turn, help to develop the interpersonal side of conversation. Thus the child's learning is related to social matters. Ideas about the world and himself (represented in the Ideational metafunction of Phase 3) become linked to the interpersonal components of language.

4. Text and Textuality

There is yet a third aspect to the development of the adult abilities of Phase 3, one which was inherent in our discussion of the other two components. Returning to a consideration of the three-part conversation between A and B, at the start of the chapter, we can now look at it from another vantage point.

If we focus on B's responses, for a moment, we realize that they do play a most important part in the dialogue. They help to bind it together, giving a smooth, cohesive exchange of personal information. This is one reason why 'response' is sometimes considered to be another type of sentence function. If it is, then 'response' operates at another linguistic level, since it can make use of question, statement or command for its purposes.

B is using her responses to maintain social cohesiveness and to keep the topic of the conversation flowing smoothly. Both Ideational and Interpersonal aspects of language are represented here. But, in addition, we should note that social cohesion is matched by linguistic cohesion, for each response is obviously linked through language to the preceding part of the conversation; it would be very odd if it didn't. This cohesion is the hallmark of what linguists call text.

In fact, any stretch of language, whether spoken or written, may be called text if its component sentences hang together. A random jumble of sentences is not text because they lack sequence and order. The sentences in a text are in a definite sequence and any alteration in their order must have an effect on the meaning and intelligibility of the whole discourse. This is perhaps more obvious in conversation, where answer must follow question and not vice versa, than it is in narrative where the speaker may make free with the order of events.

The emergence of Nigel's ability to cope with text in conversation, narrative or the stories of verbal play, showed that he had developed the textual metafunction as an integral part of coping with the other two linguistic components. In other words, he had learned to use all three language metafunctions simultaneously to produce a variety of textual material.

To illustrate what is now possible let us look again at the contrived example in which the response 'Yes, I am free, sir. Can I help you?' was found. This response takes up the implied topic or idea behind the question 'Are you free?'—namely, that help is required. In addition, it is a positive personal response. But

54

though both of these two aspects of the response use textual abilities, there is something else to notice. The responder has deliberately echoed the question, adding the title 'sir' to the utterance as well. He could have responded with a simple 'Can I help you?', for instance. Instead he chose this deliberate textual device to draw attention to the formality of his response and, by implication, to the assistant–customer relationship.

Of course, Nigel, at the start of Phase 3, was only at the beginning of learning this intricate interweaving of meanings, but he had made a start—he had developed the textual metafunction of adult language and could cope with producing and understanding a limited amount of text. He now has the rest of his life to exploit this ability, to learn the many ways of using his textual competence. In the future he will learn to read, for instance, drawing deliberately on his own language resources. As illustrated in the example above, he will come to the realization that text is structured so as to draw attention to themes and ideas or to social and personal relationships. How this is done is the subject of the next section. (30)

5. Reading and the textual metafunction

It should be apparent by now that the ability to cope with the mature language of Phase 3 requires both give and take, both the production and understanding of text. These two aspects of languaging depend on the textual metafunction, as it is this which makes text possible. The printed word, as mentioned before, is simply one form of text. It is one, of course, in which the other partner to the discourse, the reader, plays no overt part in its construction. His part is to recreate the text through the linguistic help the writer provides. Let us look briefly at the writer's structuring of text and the demands this makes on the reader's textual abilities. For the reader, these insights are part of automatic processes which rarely involve the open inspection that we are giving them here.

In the first place, linguistic analysis shows that the textual component of language helps the overall structuring of text through binding it together. Grammatical and lexical links are provided which stretch across clauses and sentences. These reinforce common-sense notions about the continuation of a topic or idea through several successive sentences. They help to draw attention to this coherence through strictly linguistic means. Here are a few examples:

Jim is my friend. *He* likes me. (Pronoun link)

Mary drove home. *Then she* had supper. (Adverbial link)

Who is it? *David, the new helper.* (Omission of elements indicates link)

The pronoun link is particularly interesting because it illustrates one very important use of pronouns in text. There are others, however, which show variations on this theme of linkage. The example given points to a linkage within the text but, often, pronouns are used to bind text with situation e.g. *He*'s the one that did *it*. *That* boy there.

Yet a third way in which pronouns are used is for social, personal linkage in binding the people to a common purpose. For instance 'Let us pray' is really a directive, but it is the 'us' which reduces the emphasis on the command, placing it instead on the joint act of worship. In producing text the writer is usually less concerned with the latter two aspects of linkage than he would be if he were speaking. All three are still there, however, and it is the reader's job to acknowledge this structuring of language.

A second, very important component that the textual meta-function gives to language is the structuring of sentences and clauses according to theme and information. Each English clause is structured to give a message. The writer or speaker draws our attention to one part of the utterance, the theme, by putting it first. Here are some examples:

THEME	REST
You	are the one.
Surprisingly	they didn't.
This	was their finest hour.

The information structure of the clause is closely associated with spoken intonation patterns or tone groups. These groups are stretches of text which have their own tune and stress. Each tune corresponds to a unit of linguistic information which is usually, though not always, a clause:

There is the man,	*I saw yesterday.*
clause 1	clause 2
information unit 1	information unit 2
'tune' 1	'tune' 2

There are two units of information in this sentence because the speaker is answering two questions, viz. Where is the man? and When did you see him? The source of both 'questions' lies in his own language resources and not in the questions posed by another person. But, ultimately, it is dialogue which develops these abilities. Monologue, narrative and writing are special cases of an implied dialogue situation. The success with which writers and readers cope with this depends in part upon conversational groundwork. This means that the good reader must be able to impose his own intonation patterns on the printed text if he is to come to a full understanding of the information it contains.

But we have not yet finished with the structuring of text, because there is the possibility of categorizing it according to topic, social situation and so on. These categories are called registers and they are important for the reader because of the lexical and grammatical predictability that they make possible. Each register acknowledges one type of relationship that exists between situation and utterance. It is a variety of a language which is distinguished by use (see Halliday, McIntosh, Strevens 1964). (32)

The topic of a register, for instance, may be recognized by the collocations of words used e.g.

> ...dribbled...wing...centred...volley...net...

These could only be taken from a football report or commentary. This recognition is not entirely a matter of lexis; grammar is involved as well. Thus with 'dribbled down the wing', 'centred the ball' and 'rammed his volley into the back of the net', each phrase has a familiarity which is the consequence of both structure and vocabulary. One supports the other in confirming the supposition that football is the topic of the description.

Another point, which has been raised by Turner (57), is that two processes are at work in the production of text. Suitable word collocations give a predictability which is useful but unexciting. The skilful language user will incorporate some unexpected words into a collocational set, both to catch our attention and to add something new to our conception of what is being described. Here we are entering the realms of the poetic and metaphorical use of words. Turner describes 'The ship coursed the seas' as a condensed riddle, for example. 'Coursed' is inappropriate to the relationship between ship and sea, but it is this very fact which draws the reader's attention. In the process of reacting with a 'Why put it like that?' question, the realization comes of the appropriateness of the physical analogy. We are thus led beyond the confines of

57

our usual responses into a world of novelty and surprise. Through his linguistic ability and creativeness the writer has enriched our experience of the physical world. We must also consider the reader's response to solving the riddle; rising, successfully, to the writer's challenge can be the source of much satisfaction.

6. Written text and reading

Putting it very generally, we may say that the process of reading is a matter of coming to terms with text in its visual form. This means, of course, that a child must rely on his own language functions just as he does in listening to spoken language. In fact, all competent language users do so, including adults who have much greater abilities. The greater these language resources, the greater the comprehension of text in all its varieties. Put like this, reading would seem to involve simply matching verbal language to its visual equivalent. But herein lies a problem; the two do not correspond perfectly.

Without going into great detail we can point to a mismatch between the basic units of speech and the writing system, the orthography. In the English language we use 26 alphabet letters to build the words of visual text. The basic units of spoken text are phonemes. These are the smallest linguistic units to carry meaningful distinctions and there are just under 50 of them. This being so there can be no 1 : 1 equivalence between sound and written form, since there are not enough letters to match each significant distinction in speech sounds. For instance the digraphs 'ch' and 'sh' represent only two speech sounds (actually, two classes of sound) despite having 4 letters between them. The point is that the basic substance of text as sound and text as writing is different, despite its equivalence for most purposes.

There are yet other difficulties, stemming from the fact that any language changes with time. The English language bears the imprint of many of the past social–historical influences upon the nation. Words of French, German, Latin, Greek origin are still apparent because their original orthography tends to be maintained largely unaltered as a result of the slow changes in the writing system. Within the orthography there are a number of sub-systems of mutually related words whose spelling rules often conflict with other groups because of their different origins. There has been no significant move towards rationalizing the position and so a child learning to read has to master an apparently inconsistent

58

spelling system. In fact, far from being a 1 : 1 system English orthography is many : many. Consider for example:

though	*ship*
bough	*sure*
trough	*chivalry*
1 written form : many phonemes	many written forms : 1 phoneme

Add to this the problem of 'silent' letters e.g. lamb, write, could,
to which there is no corresponding sound at all and the result is
not only confusion but the suspicion, in many a learner's mind,
that the odds are stacked against him.

I might add that the reverse is also true; much of spoken language is not recorded in written form. The elements of pitch, stress
and pause are very poorly recorded in writing. Punctuation may
give some help with potential speech pauses, though in practice
a speaker would sound most odd if he acknowledged just the
pauses of written text. Intonation is not involved directly and is
only incorporated in a very limited way through question and
exclamation marks. Much, therefore, of the spoken textual information is not readily apparent in written text. Its recovery depends on the reader's linguistic ability.

Finally, in terms of comprehension, a listener usually has the
immediate context of situation to aid textual interpretation. By
contrast, written text has to establish the context in which it is
set, largely through the text itself. Admittedly most children's
stories are accompanied by pictures and these are designed to give
contextual clues. However, these pictures are only as effective as
the child makes them (and this is true of the written text as well).
Verbal text, on the other hand, does not rely as heavily upon the
child's textual abilities since the subject under discussion is usually
readily apparent. Even if it is not, the speaker can, through his
own abilities, adjust to the needs of his listener and the circumstances. A writer is much more limited in this respect.

6 Reading and listening

'Reading is not primarily a visual process.'

Frank Smith

1. Introduction

For the mature language user, reading and listening are 'passive' activities. They demand that a person's potentiality for active language involvement be set aside, however temporarily, in favour of a spectator's role. Not that this is a passive activity in the sense of receptively uninvolved; the mind is not a *tabula rasa* to be written upon freely. Both activities make great demands upon personal involvement because an individual's language abilities must be actively engaged prior to, as well as during, the analysis of particular stretches of text. Prediction must precede analysis if efficient processing is to result.

Participation is then a key word in the description of all language activities, including reading and listening. The extraction of meaning from any piece of text depends very much on the individual. What he knows, what strategies he employs, in what manner he employs his abilities, these are all matters of some importance in this context. Personality, natural ability, as well as the opportunities and circumstances for learning, are interweaving factors in the development of mature language abilities.

In fact, one does not have to search particularly hard to find very striking similarities between these two processes of reading and listening. This is not surprising, as both textual substances, spoken and written words, are the product of language construction, but nonetheless the degree of similarity is greater than the differences between the two forms might lead one to suppose. Despite these differences the individual's task in processing both is the same: to use his own language abilities to effect the maximum degree of comprehension. It can be pointed out, quite rightly, that the oral form precedes the visual both historically and in the development of each person. It would seem more appropriate, however, to regard the two as parallel as far as mature language processing is concerned. This may seem relatively unimportant, but it does have serious implications for the attack on reading problems.

At present, much reading instruction places heavy emphasis on 'decoding to sound', that is converting print to spoken language. In fact, many experts in linguistics and education have used the idea of such a process in their definitions of reading e.g. Bloomfield (9) and Gibson (25). By this token, reading becomes a two-stage process: Stage 1 consists of decoding the visual text to sound and Stage 2 is the analysis of the sound for its linguistic content. But such ideas fly in the face of what we know about reading. For the proficient reader, at any rate, resorting to sound is a last, not a first, resort. Besides, it is not necessary to postulate an intermediate sound stage between visual text and meaning; one can be translated into the other much more directly. The individual's language abilities are being used, of course, but on visual not derived oral text.

In the following sections we will look at what the skilled reader and listener is actually doing in coping with the perceptual problems of text. Then the part that language plays in these activities will be discussed. But, before we embark upon these tasks, a word of explanation is necessary about the choice of describing the skilled, proficient processor of text rather than a remedial child.

The principal reason is that it is important to know the techniques and abilities which bring success. I have attempted to demonstrate in previous chapters that the emphasis on failure has not been helpful, either to the children concerned or to the genesis of appropriate theory. There is a need to shift to theory which will underpin learning success. From this point of view, we need to look at successful techniques to see how the fluent reader and the competent listener cope with their difficulties. With this information we can then return to the remedial child to assess how he is attempting to cope with text. Hopefully, we will be able to increase the efficiency of what he is trying to do through the knowledge we have gained in looking at mature techniques.

A second point is that the information gleaned from expert practitioners constitutes a much better touchstone of what reading is about than what is obtained from the study of poor readers. The norm-oriented and specific learning difficulty approaches, I have argued, have tended to obscure relevant issues. By focusing instead on learning, and not on deviations from the average, we may hope to correct this bias.

2. The skilled listener

What, first of all, is the skilled listener doing when he processes spoken text? A first answer is that he is probably attempting to cope with the normal utterance rate of ten phonemes (distinctive speech sounds) per second. (20) This is an incredible performance when one considers that the sure identification of all sounds individually would take many times longer. Of course, listening to isolated language sounds is artificial and is not part of the listener's usual repertoire, but it does indicate that the process employed is not one of listening for individual sounds. What the skilled listener does is to employ his linguistic knowledge to group and segment the utterance in particular ways. On a statistical basis, for instance, certain phonemes are heard more frequently than others and so are particular combinations and orders of sounds. This is one source of knowledge the listener can employ. Another, at the meaningful level, is the interpretation of new sentences using the notion of abstract grammatical–logical relationships such as actor, process and goal.

As Fry has pointed out (22), the decoding of speech is a twofold process in which the listener receives acoustic information from an outside source and combines it with his own linguistic information. Exactly what mix of information is used depends on a person's ability and the conditions under which the transaction takes place. Noisy surroundings will put a premium on language anticipations and guesswork. It is worth noting that only 60–80% of any sustained conversation is usually heard by the listener, anyway. (17) There is no awareness of any hiatus, because language anticipations automatically fill in what one supposes to be missing. In any case, it is neither necessary nor efficient to listen to all the acoustic information, even if it were possible. The sensible thing, which the listener does undertake, is to select and ignore so that he may overcome processing restrictions. He proceeds on the assumption that the utterance is constrained in a meaningful way by its linguistic patterns. This is the view of Wiener, who has written (quoted by Fry (22)) that 'the most important thing we can know about a message is that it makes sense'. Every listener has to work with this assumption.

3. The skilled reader

The skilled reader employs, not surprisingly, very similar abilities and processes. The average college student, for instance, reads about 300 words per minute, or 5 words per second. Putting the average word between 4–6 letters long, this makes a processing rate of 20–30 letters every second. But we know from experiments on visual perception that the identification of an individual letter takes longer than $\frac{1}{4}$ second. This would give a maximum processing rate of about 4 letters a second, barely enough to identify one word, let alone five. Yet five words a second is modest by some standards. Proficient speed readers may attain a reading rate of 1,000 words per minute, with no apparent diminution in comprehension. I leave the reader to calculate the incredible word and letter processing rate (per second) that such abilities must require.

What is readily discernible is that reading cannot proceed through a letter by letter sequential processing and identification method. Paul Kolers (38) demonstrated this quite nicely by showing people the letters of words very rapidly in sequence. His subjects found word identification by this method very difficult. The reader, like the listener, must have access to other information that will enable him to process the substance of the text for the visual information that enables letter identification to be avoided. That information, of course, comes from the individual's own linguistic resources. Just how language affects our reading perception may be judged from the classic studies undertaken by Cattell. (13) He showed that, in one single brief exposure, a skilled reader could identify either 4–5 unconnected letters or 2 unconnected words or a phrase or sentence of 4–5 words. In other words, the more linguistically organized the material the greater the apprehension span in terms of letters.

Other studies have added to our knowledge of the more physical aspects of reading. Reading requires continuous activity in the form of eye movements, although the reader cannot process print efficiently when the eyes are in motion. What happens is that the eyes move jerkily and not smoothly. In between movements, the visual material is fixated briefly so that, in effect, the whole process adds up to a successive sampling of the text. The eye does not scan along a row of letters in order to identify a word, but takes in all the relevant information more or less simultaneously. This helps to explain why Kolers's subjects found the successive presentation of letters so difficult a task.

As with all the processes we have studied so far, we may point to the involvement of language in reading progress. In this case, the linguistic interaction is similar to what Cattell uncovered. Through language involvement the skilled reader processes more in a single glance than either a poor reader or a more immature one. What he does is to use his language abilities efficiently, thus extending the number of letters and words processed in the time. The skilled reader uses only as much visual information as he requires to confirm his language predictions, and so a full analysis of the printed word is not required. The reader samples just enough of the word, visually, to check whether it matches what he supposes to be there.

We get further evidence of anticipatory language involvement from eye–voice studies. In reading aloud, it is quite evident that the fluent reader scans ahead with his eyes to sample what he has to say. The extent to which this is done may be assessed by cutting off the visual information suddenly (e.g. turning the light off) and noting how many words of the text the reader continues to utter. The skilled reader is usually 3–5 words ahead of his voice, about one second's worth at the normal reading rate.

The principal characteristic, then, of the skilled reader is the fluency and speed with which he processes text. We have seen that this fluency is related to anticipatory linguistic abilities, which allow the reader to sample part of the visual information instead of processing the text in its entirety. As with listening, the reader works with the assumption that he is dealing with meaningful material. Without this assumption and its subsequent validation there would be no reason to attempt textual predictions, because he would not be expecting rule-governed utterances. The corollary to this argument is that predictions are not only constrained by linguistic rules in a general sense but also by individual linguistic abilities. Skilled reading is an active reconstruction of text, depending on the adult language abilities that were described in the previous chapter. Skilled reading represents one application of the developed language system—the turning point of which was the inception of the textual function into the child's language capabilities.

4. Some theoretical considerations

In this section of the chapter I intend to pursue the topics raised by the consideration of skilled listening and reading to a more theoretical and, possibly, more controversial level. What I have to write (and have already written) owes much to a seminal group of papers and articles assembled by Frank Smith. (54) These have laid the foundation of a more enlightened approach to reading and its difficulties. They also go some way towards solving the dilemma that Ulric Neisser has brought to our attention. He has written: 'Unless some understanding of reading for meaning is achieved we will remain embarrassingly ignorant about questions that appear superficially easy ... For the present, rapid reading represents an achievement as impossible in theory as it is commonplace in practice.' (46) Similar difficulties have confronted the theorists concerned with listening skills.

There are two principal themes to pursue: The categorization of textual stimuli i.e. printed letters, words, and the integration of these textual stimuli with the individual's own linguistic system. The two themes are not really separate; they represent two different emphases, two aspects of developing textual competence.

One major school of thought has it (11) that a stimulus is identified when it is allocated to a particular category or class of stimuli. For instance, in looking at the letter 'a', we may classify it, first, as an alphabet letter, secondly, as one of 26 letters of the English alphabet and, finally, as one example of the class of letter 'a's which may be written in a number of ways. This classification must be an intellectual act since the selection process relies on the use of knowledge to match stimulus with the abstract category. By implication, the decision process eliminates the other alternative processes as well. In recognizing the letter 'a', the reader is also saying, 'This visual configuration is not one of the other 25 classes of alphabet letters.'

Similar reasoning is used to account for the identification of individual phonemes when listening to auditory stimuli. Here we have proof of linguistic influences which affect auditory perception. It has been shown, for example, that a listener's discriminative powers are not constant but vary with the characteristics of the speech sounds they are processing. (40) Maximum sensitivity is found at the boundaries between phonemic classes, for instance on the boundary between the similar /b/ and /g/ sounds. In other words, we learn to employ our discriminative abilities most effectively where there is ambiguity and the greater possibility of error. Where the physical characteristics of a speech sound put it firmly within one class, there is no need to use full perceptual abilities. Over a period of time this differential use of discriminative powers leads to the learned differences that Liberman found.

A parallel view of visual perceptual processes has been adopted by Eleanor Gibson. (24) The basis for this argument is that each physical stimulus is considered to be a bundle of combined features. We learn to identify a particular phoneme or letter by abstracting these individualistic features from the stimuli. Each feature is not exclusive to that letter but, in combination with other features, helps towards positive identification. For example, the letter 'd' shares the closed part of its shape, one of its features, with the letters 'o' and 'a'. Add the vertical line, another feature, and four letters 'b', 'p', 'd', 'q' are possible. The up-down feature separates 'b', 'd' from 'p', 'q' and, finally, the left-right feature separates 'd' from 'b'. No one feature is exclusive to the letter 'd' and its identification, therefore, depends on recognizing a combination (bundle) of features.

The ability to cope with distinctive features is learned through employing perceptual, linguistic and intellectual abilities. Initially, the reader/listener learns that he is working with only a limited number of categories (e.g. 26 letters) and that this fact can be used to reduce the complexity of his task. He organizes his perceptual system to deal with the significant contrasts between categories. He learns also to group sounds or letters together because they contrast meaningfully within a given context. To realize that 'pin' and 'pen' have different referents is also to acknowledge a category of 'vowels' in which /i/ and /e/ may be contrasted. Similar arguments can be raised for other auditory and visual contrasts. Through organizing the categories into similar groupings, the reader/listener is reducing the perceptual processing even further. Given, say, the recognition that a letter must be a vowel, he need only search through those contrasts which distinguish the vowels—a great reduction in processing.

Through meaning, perception becomes a search for significant pointers to aid identification. But, as will be appreciated, the description of the processing has to account more and more for contextual influences and relative evaluation. We take cognizance of the information that has already been processed from the text. Through what has been spoken or written, and by application of our linguistic knowledge, we can limit further the amount of

66

visual or auditory information we need for identification. For instance, prediction of words becomes easier the longer a clause or sentence goes on. Knowing the initial words helps considerably. What this means is that grammatical and meaningful constraints exercise a progressive influence, by reducing the number of alternatives that may be expected. The listener may be left with a decision between 'din' or 'bin' (Is it /d/ or /b/?) or between 'dot' and 'lot' (Is it /d/ or /l/?) and so on. All that is needed to complete word identification, under these circumstances, is to search for those contrasts which indicate the difference between these pairs of sounds (or letters, for visual text) which the context has shown to be likely. The distinctive features vary, therefore, with the particular comparison involved.

The final stage of this development is when only minimum cues are needed for all the letters or sounds in a word. Identification of the word, at this stage, is a matter of confirming the expected. In other words, we are using a processing system in which the linguistic information is at a maximum. It is supposed that if the visual or auditory information actually used in this system was employed on its own, then no constituent letter or sound would be identified.

Such a state of affairs may seem slightly odd, but then there are some facts which are very difficult to explain by any other means. Take, for instance, some of the experimental evidence on identification thresholds for visually presented words. (34) It is well known, and to be expected, that the identification of a word in context is faster than the identification time for a word on its own. In a highly probable context the recognition of the word is even faster. The other physical manifestation of this contextual help can be demonstrated by varying the illumination of the target word. Under these circumstances the word in context is recognized at lower thresholds than the individual word in isolation.

Neither of these results is particularly surprising. However, the fact that words are often recognized when not one of the letters can be picked out, may be. Similar evidence has been reported by Worthington (62) in an experiment where his subjects did not know they were dealing with verbal stimuli. In the experiment the subjects were sat in a dark room and told to press a button when they could see a white light of variable intensity. What they did not know was that the light was a disc with a word printed on it. Various words were used and none were reported seen by the subjects. Worthington used both emotionally neutral words together with some obscene ones. The interesting fact to emerge was that the light-intensity threshold of the disc with an obscene word on it was much higher than for a neutral word. The subjects were reacting to the meaning of the words in circumstances where they were not aware of the words themselves. The supposition must be that there was sufficient visual information to start engaging automatic linguistic activities, but not enough for word identification. Such explanations may help to explain the somewhat enigmatic statement by Smith (54) that comprehension precedes the identification of words and not vice versa.

Finally, a brief word about another physical aspect of reading, mentioned previously in the chapter. This was the ability of the skilled reader to process several words at a single fixation of the eyes. We know from the work on short-term memory (44) that there are processing limits to the information that an individual can take in at a time. How, then, is it possible to recognize 4–5 words when only 4–5 unconnected letters may be identified in the same time? The answer is that the same amount of visual information is taken in both cases. What varies is the amount of linguistic information which the reader uses to supplement it. The greater the linguistic information the more thinly need the visual information be spread over the letters and words. Conversely, the less the linguistic organization of the material or the individual, the greater the emphasis on the visual aspects of word identification.

For both listener and reader, it is language abilities and the way in which these are used that determines what text can be coped with proficiently. This involves sampling and predicting, in order to use the least amount of stimulus information. This ability to predict is, of course, a function of the individual's textual proficiency.

7 Learning to read

'We are all of us learning to read all the time.'

I. A. Richards

1. Introduction

In the previous chapter we saw how mature reading abilities depend on the interaction between visual and non-visual sources of information. The latter is very largely linguistic, depending on the individual's ability and experience. The amount of language involvement governs both the number of words fixed at a given moment and the speed of reading. Linguistic and visual sources of information are, in fact, inversely related in reading. For instance, where linguistic involvement is limited, a much greater emphasis is placed upon the visual system. As a consequence the word span lessens to accommodate for these changes.

This balance between linguistic and visual processes is a sensitive one which responds both to changes in text and in the individual's ability to cope with it. Even the proficient reader may be slowed to a snail's pace by difficult unfamiliar text, such as articles on geomorphology or genetics. Conversely, the young inexperienced reader can read a familiar story such as *Beauty and the Beast* very quickly, particularly when there are ritual phrases in it like 'once upon a time' and 'lived happily ever after'.

It is not surprising, therefore, to find a positive relationship between linguistic accomplishments and reading at all ages. For instance, Ruth Strickland (55) found a relationship between silent reading comprehension and the structure of children's oral language. The pupils who were ranked high in reading comprehension were the ones who used particular structures more frequently and who used longer utterances more often. In slightly different

69

vein, Ruddell showed that comprehension scores were higher when children read from passages in which the written structural patterns resembled their own oral language. (52)

The relationship of language to reading is such that one can be tied in with the other over considerable periods of time. A correlation has been reported (58) between children's speech at $2\frac{1}{2}$ years and reading comprehension at 8 years. Furthermore, a 'Tell-a-story' technique is now available for use with young children which exploits this kind of relationship. The number of words children use in outlining a story from a set of pictures gives useful predictions of future reading difficulties. (33)

It may be, as Vernon has suggested (58), that language and reading abilities match fairly well for most children, but not for those with reading problems. If this is so, then the way the two abilities develop is crucial to the child in terms of both academic and personal status. When the integration of the visual and linguistic information systems is inefficient the result must be to reduce reading progress to a slow pace. This, in turn, must affect language development too. As James Britton has written:

'to succeed in making sense of a text containing unfamiliar words is the normal way of enlarging one's linguistic resources. In other words, it is from reading (or more completely from reading and listening, reinforced by talking and writing), that we learn to interpret the various contributions that a given word may make to the meaning of an utterance.' (10)

2. The development of reading abilities

There is, as I have regretted before, little in the way of substantiated theory to guide our thoughts on the more particular aspects of reading development. What follows is an attempt to rough in the outlines of how developing language abilities are used to create greater ability to make sense of written text. The process, of course, is not simply an additive one but multiplicative, with each aspect of textual ability, both visual and auditory, feeding the process of the other.

The development of the auditory aspect of text extends back to the second year of a child's life and forward to maturity and old age. Its use is more or less continuous throughout this time because our lives revolve around verbal exchange and communication. Progress, under normal circumstances, is also continuous, matching the developing uses of language.

70

The involvement with visual text develops later and is much more deliberate. On the one hand we talk of a child learning language and, on the other, of being taught to read. The contrast in attitude towards the two processes is most marked and may have some bearing upon the past emphasis on reading and the comparative neglect of linguistic issues. But there is another important difference too. It is very difficult to avoid linguistic processing and involvement in the auditory sphere, but only too easy with visual text. We only have to close our eyes, look in another direction or avoid particular situations and we are able, with very little difficulty, to avoid reading as well. The individual has a much greater chance of opting out in this respect, though he becomes much more conspicuous educationally for doing so.

The child's first introduction to visual text is often when mother or father sits with him to read stories. This is simply an extension of a developing interest in the narrative mode of language interaction, which has involved story telling as well as listening to stories. At this point the integration of language and visual processes begins, together with the employment of knowledge and other cognitive abilities. As Britton has said, in a slightly different context, the most relevant processes which a reader brings to the task of reading are the conscious expectations of what it is about. (10) Judged on this basis the transition from being read to— to starting the process for himself, must be an important period for the child. During this time he probably learns of the connection between visual and auditory text, between the printed story and the spoken language. In other words the child learns that what he knows, and uses already, is appropriate to the activity of reading. He must learn, too, that, although he must engage these textual abilities, there are differences between the verbal and visual forms which have to be taken into consideration. The reader is referred to the final section of chapter 5 for a previous discussion of this topic.

Of course, all children are exposed to a lot of print in their surroundings and some learn quite a lot from television adverts, shop signs, the tins in mother's cupboard and so on. From the point of view of starting to learn to read, this is fine but it suffers from the handicap of being very haphazard stimulation. Rather like the corresponding stage in language development in which the child 'gets the idea' of naming objects, what is important is to build this interest into a grammatical system so that what has been learned can be used in a multiplicity of linguistic utterances. The same applies here; what is important to the child is not just the realization that familiar objects are associated with printed words, but that these printed words are put together to form a linguistic system.

3. Word identification

The focus upon the individual word is a useful point of departure in discussing the development of reading since I have already discussed letter identification. Our first concern will be with the dual aspects of word recognition and word learning, though, at times, there is no clear demarcation between the two. This is because 'recognition' can be used in the sense of realizing that a visual configuration corresponds to a unit in the language system. The child can say, in effect, 'that must be the word "apple" because it starts ap... and the word "apple" fits the context'. Since the child does not recognize the visual form of the word immediately, yet has come to a realization of what it represents, he must be in the process of learning it. In this case recognition and learning are not separable; recognition is the means by which learning takes place. But recognition has another sense, too, as it can be used to describe the process of classifying events or objects or attributes as being the same in two distinct and separate instances. One can say 'that is the same car I saw yesterday' without knowing the make or type. In other words one can recognize on the basis of visual matching alone and in the absence of further information about the stimuli. In reading, such abilities indicate progress in moving off the bottom rungs of the ladder. The child is improving when he can recognize that a word has been seen before, though without necessarily knowing what it means.

Prior to this stage the child must have the ability to recognize words visually over very short time durations. He needs enough information, that is, to say 'same' or 'different' with some confidence when presented with pairs of words. To do this the child must abstract some of the word's features (see previous chapter) in order to compare with the next example. Of course, the child has to learn what to abstract and will, therefore, tend to make a lot of errors in doing so. Adults often see these errors as 'silly mistakes' because they can't see why the child isn't using word-recognition strategies that are second nature to them. But this is precisely what the child is trying to do; he is learning to apply what he knows as efficiently as possible. His job is to identify words

72

on the minimum number of clues, which are principally visual at this time.

At this stage of development language plays a crucial role in forming good reading habits. In one sense what the child produces as guesses for particular words is not so important because these represent various visual hypotheses which can be adjusted. What is vital is that the child should realize how close he is in a guess to the actual word. Such information comes from the child's own linguistic knowledge which must be applied to the stretch of language and not just to the guessed word. 'That word doesn't fit because it doesn't make sense', must be the reasoning. With this kind of feedback the child can then make adjustments to the initial hypotheses and strategies. In this way progress is made and the child learns to regulate his own reading by reading 'for sense'.

Just what strategies a child adopts varies with the child concerned and with the material he is called on to process. The latter is often tied fairly closely to some method of teaching reading, such as 'look and say', 'phonic' and 'whole sentence' methods. The fact is that most children are fairly robust as regards reading methods. They learn to read whichever one is employed. The crucial issue is not what concept of reading underlies the construction of the text, but whether a child can cope with the language used. If the child can match his own linguistic abilities against the visual text, then the basis for progress is there.

With greater reading experience, word identification changes in character. In the first place, the linguistic feedback on the reading process leads to greater visual knowledge, based upon language constraints. We learn, for instance, that the sequence 'str' is possible and 'srt' is not, that 'str' is most likely to start a word, is less likely in the middle and is not found at all as the end three letters. We apply this kind of information in identifying and learning new words. The second kind of change is that language abilities play a greater part in the hypothesis stage of word identification. More and more the child uses its textual knowledge to project what word he expects to find, thus taking the emphasis off the reliance on visual information which was apparent early on. Not only does the child learn to use abilities in this respect more effectively as time progresses, but the textual ability itself is developed at the same time.

When children start reading they usually rely on supplementary help in addition to their developing textual abilities. For this reason primers, and other early reading books, lean heavily on illustration to convey part of the information about the text. This contextual help supplies the child with pictorial representations to bind the story theme to the print. In addition, each picture may suggest that particular items of vocabulary will be present in the story. Alternatively, the child may use the picture to confirm an idea or a guessed word. By this two-way information flow, of picture-to-text and text-to-picture, the child builds up his experience of visual text. As he does so, he comes to rely more heavily on the text itself for vocabulary hypotheses, first through the word in its sentence frame and, later, through the textual influences that the other sentences supply. At this point pictorial help is probably unnecessary.

We may represent the development of word identification and related abilities as follows:

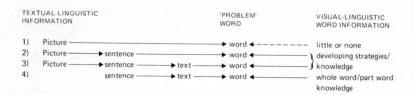

In fact, there is another stage beyond the last represented here. At Stage 4 above, the child has got to the point when the problem word can be identified entirely through the combination of information from the text and personal word and textual knowledge. Sufficient visual information has to be present to enable some form of visual word identification to take place, even though the emphasis is now on the linguistic side in reading.

The final stage is when no individual word identification is necessary, when reading is completely smooth. Here the visual information used is below that necessary for visual identification of a word. It is used simply to supplement and confirm the linguistic information which is in the form of anticipatory hypotheses. In other words visual information is being mapped directly on to meaning.

4. Word experience

So far I have deliberately avoided a discussion of reading instruction and teacher/parent help. This is because I want to represent reading, from the child's point of view, as a self-directed process for the most part. Such a view is obviously somewhat at odds with what actually happens. In word identification, for instance, a fair proportion of visual knowledge is built up initially through the child being told the words he does not know. While this is true, I regard this form of instruction as potentially unhelpful to many children. The reason is that it short-cuts the processing of words to the detriment of the developing visual–linguistic word knowledge. Such an argument harks back to what I wrote earlier in the chapter about understanding that visual text, with its printed words, is another linguistic system. The point is that, if the child is simply told a word, the linguistic information is then associated with whatever visual information has been processed however irrelevant that may have been. By this 'help' the visual and linguistic systems may be linked in a most haphazard manner, resulting in the eventual confusion of the child. Obviously, such considerations are not of great importance to many children who are otherwise processing text for themselves satisfactorily. Where these assume greater significance is for the children who are having initial difficulties coming to terms with print.

Another facet of adult intervention concerns the reading material that is selected for the child to read. We cannot go far without coming across the great phonic versus look–say debate. Not that these represent the only two methods of reading instruction, but they have been the two most influential. Since both are based upon the supposed effective development of word knowledge and experience, it is convenient to discuss them briefly at this point.

The look–say approach aims to establish a working sight vocabulary from the start. Children are taught to recognize a limited number of words by associating the sound with the printed word on a flashcard. These learned words are then used as the basis for the initial stories of the reading series. Additional words are added later, and phonic instruction may be included, but essentially the method aims to teach children on a whole-word basis. In this it is the shape of the whole word which is thought to give the child the ability to discriminate the different words.

The phonic method, on the other hand, aims to teach letter–sound correspondence so that unknown words can be built up from their constituent sounds. The emphasis at the start is on letters and on producing letter sounds. It is not concerned with whole word shapes.

But how do these approaches tally with what we have already discovered about reading? Leaving aside the fact that both result in incredibly stilted reading primers with little resemblance to natural language, we find there are differences from what would seem to encourage efficient reading processes. Not that these cannot be developed; they just seem to make the child's job that bit harder. By teaching word–sound associations out of context, for instance, one is encouraging the inefficient use of visual clues. The instantaneous recognition of words is the last step in the development of good reading habits not the first. By excluding linguistic involvement to a large degree the child is being cut off from those abilities which he would normally employ. The result is an uninspired word guesser, the typical victim of such starvation.

There must be comparable reservations about the phonic method as well. As I have said, word identification does not, and cannot, proceed on a letter by letter basis. In addition, children left to themselves do very little spontaneous sounding out of letters. Apart from the difficulty of additional intrusive sounds ('b' says 'buh') there is the problem that the isolated letter sounds do not blend together to make the sound of the target word. The child has to make an intellectual adjustment in order to make sense of the data. It is like expecting a child to swim having practised the separate leg and arm movements in isolation. Besides this one cannot go far without hitting further snags, which include the huge number of phonic rules that are needed to account for all correspondences. In fact, the teaching of phonics is usually much more limited in its aim, confining itself to a few of the 'regular' rules.

Of course, the child, developing word experience, has to work on the assumption that there are visual–sound links which will aid his processing. In other words, he makes use of simple letter–sound correspondences, though rarely sounding them out. Letter identification is a prerequisite to such activity and, later, so is the identification of letter sequences. But the child soon learns that the identification of all the letters in a word is not necessary, anyway, as he can combine linguistic information with phonic analysis to identify the difficult words. This helps to avoid the difficulties posed by 'irregular' words and the problem of which phonic rules to apply in particular circumstances.

But, as word experience grows, other difficulties appear in the form of more complex words with larger numbers of letters. These bring additional problems, besides the previous phonic ones, since they involve two or more syllables and the complication of stress. How would a child cope with the difference beween '*comp*act' (noun—referring to an agreement between parties) and 'com*pact*' (adjective—referring to the neatness or closeness of objects) if it were not for linguistic knowledge? You must know what a word is in order to get its stress pattern right.

It is at this stage that the child has to abandon its original hypothesis of sound–letter correspondences in favour of a letter–meaning one. Our spelling system (or systems, if you prefer) is geared to preserve the visual similarities between words that are meaningfully linked e.g. the visual aspects of 'nation' and 'nationality' clearly indicate a common origin which is not preserved by the alteration in vowel and stress of the word sounds. The more experienced reader starts to make implicit use of this kind of visual knowledge in selecting visual analogies for unknown words, though there are still problems. For instance, knowing 'nation' and 'ration' how does one pronounce 'station'? Only reference to further linguistic knowledge can answer this question.

5. Meaning

Another aspect to reading development is the acknowledgement of meaningful stretches of text. This relates to intonation, pauses and clause structure, a topic which was dealt with in Chapter 5 when the information structure of text was discussed. Here I want to discuss briefly the development of this ability in relation to short-term memory and processing restrictions.

The proficient reader starts by learning to produce the intonation patterns of different types of short simple sentences. He finally moves on to longer sentences with two or more clauses which require reading in phrases, together with suitable pauses. This ability must obviously be related to the development of his own verbal textual abilities, together with accruement of knowledge about the world at large.

We have already discussed the relationship of language to word span and the fact that language makes it possible to take in more print at an instant. Language is the means by which visual processing limitations are circumvented. What are these restrictions and how do they affect reading? There appears to be a limitation to the amount of information the brain can handle at any given moment. For instance, most adults can remember about 7 numbers in sequence, presented at one per second. In young children the memory span is smaller by about half and this therefore places greater constraints on processing. The way memory span affects reading is by dictating the maximum number of chunks of print, either words or letters, which can be used at a time. In fact, we know that adult readers do not work to their maximum of 6–7 words when reading out loud. Eye–voice span and eye fixation span give the number as 4–5 words at a time. For younger children on a 3–4 chunk memory span, say, their word capability is probably 1 or 2 words at a time. Given this kind of limitation the linguistic involvement, in the form of anticipatory responses and comprehension, must be similarly restricted. As textual abilities increase so will memory span and reading abilities. This will be evidenced by the greater number of words processed at a time.

The development of meaning involves language, thinking and knowledge. For the child it is a matter of bringing these abilities and attainments to the reading task and being enriched in the process. Initially the child's experience of processes in the world around him, his conceptualization of objects and attributes and his linguistic experience are somewhat limited. However, they are vital to reading progress and, if applied appropriately, make a tremendous difference to reading attainments. The child who makes use of context, such as story pictures, in the early stages is the superior reader later. (15) As the contextual props are gradually pulled away, the child has to use the text increasingly as his source of information. Through it he combines his linguistic abilities and knowledge to sort out the meaning of unfamiliar words. In this way his textual abilities are broadened as is his experience. Eventually he will have access not only to the information conveyed by the text itself but also to implications that the author has used in building the story. Take this opening line from a story, for instance:

'1944; a winter's night, when only vestiges of cloud brushed across the face of the moon.'

Without being explicit the author has conveyed (or attempted to) the implication that the scene is set in wartime on a moonlit night. But this is only accessible to those with knowledge and ability. The child needs to know about the second world war and its dates. Linguistic knowledge plays its part, too, since it is from experience of text that we realize that the introduction of a date marks significant information for the later part of the narrative. Besides this the child is called upon to reason that if there isn't much cloud then the moon will be shining. Even if he doesn't know the meaning of the word 'vestiges' his linguistic ability should tell him that 'only' in 'only vestiges of cloud' signals a small amount. Hence the logical deduction is still open to him.

But, apart from these first-order implications, there are second and third order ones (and so on) that may be employed as the story progresses. For instance, the two initial implications may be combined to give a third: the possibility that the story is about a raid—in fact, it is about a bombing raid. Clearly to extract this much from text one has to employ all ones knowledge and ability; nothing less will do. In Goodman's words: 'In every act of reading, the reader draws on the sum total of prior experience and learning.' (26)

8 Assessment reconsidered

'There is no reading problem. There are problem teachers and problem schools.'

Herbert Kohl (37)

1. Introduction

Whatever else one may think of it, Herbert Kohl's provocative statement is a potent reminder that the implications of reading help and assessment are not quite as straightforward as they might seem. The usual implications concern the child, what he is doing and how he has developed this present method of working. But Kohl reminds us that, as well, there are other implications concerning the school and the teachers who have taught the child. If the child is not reading well, then we must all examine our consciences.

But for a teacher, particularly, the assessment of a child is a fresh opportunity. First, it is essential to find out what the child is *actually* doing and not what one supposes he is doing. Second, such information provides the chance of assessing the effects of previous help, as well as providing the incentive to plan for the future. Unless this kind of tactic is adopted we waste the opportunity of a realistic approach to developing reading.

2. Reading tests

It has been usual to start the assessment of reading abilities through one of the established reading tests. These translate what the child scores into a reading age, which tells the assessor that the child's abilities are equivalent to the average child of a particular age.

There are, in fact, a number of different sorts of reading test to choose from. First of all, there is the 'list' type where a number of increasingly difficult words are presented as a list. The number of words read correctly is taken as the reading score. Next comes the 'sentence' type where the material is presented in the form of increasingly difficult sentences. Here it is the number of sentences read correctly which gives the reading score. Yet another sort of test uses short stories of graded difficulty. In this type it is the number of errors which forms the basis for scoring. Other intermediate types exist as well. For instance, it is possible to combine the 'sentence' and 'list' types.

All of the above types require the assessor to listen to the reading performance of the child individually. There are others, however, which require the child to read to himself, silently, and to respond appropriately to what he reads. This type is suitable for administration to groups. One example is the underlining of one of four alternatives to fit a sentence frame. The following illustrates this type of silent reading test approach:

The cat was chased by the (dig, *dog*, god, dock).

Now all of these different tests recognize, if only implicitly, varying hypotheses of what reading is about. Let us now examine them in a little more detail so that we may see what aspects they stress and how that compares to the way reading has been preserved in this book.

First of all, we can see that the word list is a fairly quick method of assessing reading capabilities individually. It puts very strong emphasis on the visual identification of words in isolation, a kind of look–say test. By using the words without the structure of sentence or text for support, what is actually being tested is word knowledge and not the reading process itself. Of course, word experience is quite a useful guide to the amount of reading processing which has gone on, but it does not show how the difficult word is tackled in a story.

By contrast, all the other tests do use stretches of language, either sentences or text, as the material to read. They are, therefore, in a position to look beyond isolated word identification to the effects of linguistic structure and meaning on reading. Admittedly, the sentence type is limited to within-sentence constraints, but it does introduce language into the test situation. Unfortunately, this insight is usually thrown away by awarding marks on the basis of reading the whole sentence correctly.

The two types of reading test which involve the greatest use of language and meaning are those using text and silent reading comprehension. Where text is used, there is the greatest opportunity for a full analysis of the child's reading techniques. Not surprisingly it is one such, the Neale Analysis of Reading Abilities (45), that offers the fullest on-the-spot analysis of what the child is doing. The others that have been discussed so far have to rely on additional tests to pinpoint actual difficulties. Neale's test does build such information into the reading situation itself. My criticism of it is that the analysis is limited to cataloguing errors, often at one step removed from the problem. One records the occurrence of omissions, reversals, substitutions and so on. This actually gives far more detail than any other of the types discussed, but at an abstracted level which recognizes certain classes of error but not the processes by which they were made or other relevant details. As a consequence, the categories in the analysis are set up, on what is immediately apparent to the observer. This means that a reversal error such as 'saw' for 'was' is recorded but not whether the error is corrected. The latter is a very important detail.

Such a bias is to be expected from the way the test is administered. The assessor has to sit and listen to the reading performance, while marking errors as they occur. In these conditions, processing and time limitations mean that the analysis has to be restricted to those things which are easily observable.

Finally, the silent reading test is completely different to all the others in not requiring an audible reading performance. In this respect it is most like normal reading procedures as a child can demonstrate an ability to get meaning out of text, which, if read aloud, would have posed considerable problems. The other side to this coin is that one has very little idea of what is going on and what precise difficulties the child is experiencing. A less important problem is the hiding of difficulties through random guesswork. In the example above the child has a 1 : 4 chance of getting the correct answer, 'dog', by picking an answer with a pin.

3. Reading analysis

The principal criticism of reading tests is that, by and large, their objectives are monumentally irrelevant. They are concerned to derive reading ages when they should be concerned with reading.

A reading age tells you nothing of how a child is actually reading or how you should proceed in encouraging reading development In any case, reading aloud, which most tests demand, is a different task to reading to oneself, silently. This is part of observer–participant differences in language, related to processing restrictions. A participant is much more constrained by the nature of the material to be processed and responded to. An observer, on the other hand, is freer to interpret and explore the meaningful possibilities of the physical stimuli. One can focus on the physical detail to the detriment of overall description or vice-versa. It all depends on how one wants to handle the information (assuming one has a choice).

To ask a child to read aloud is to ask him to focus on the mechanistic details of reading and to reduce meaningful information. On the other hand, silent reading gives the assessor no knowledge of how the reader is undertaking the process, though it gives better information on what he understands. One solution to the dilemma is to use two different tests—one silent, one reading aloud—though the previous objections may be raised once again. The other solution, I would suggest, is to adopt an entirely different approach by using a tape recorder. By tape recording a child one may get the best of a number of worlds. In the first place, one can then analyse the reading performance in depth and at one's leisure. This means that one avoids both the difficulty of analysing reading as it happens and the tendency towards impulsive judgement. In fact, the assessor need not be present at all, if the child is competent to handle the tape recorder.

The second benefit is that no special test material is required as the emphasis is on the analysis of the child's reading processes and not on the scores relating to reading age and averages. This has the added advantage that the technique can be used as part of the normal classroom reading process. I shall take up this point in the next chapter. Not only can the technique be used to benefit classroom activities, but the situation can be reversed in that the continuing use of this procedure supplements the original assessment. It enables the teacher to provide continuous assessment, thereby avoiding the need for the occasional test, the source of so much discomfort for those under the 'magnifying glass'.

Yet another advantage is that one can test the child's understanding of what he has read by playing the tape recording back with the child listening and following in the book. This second run through enables you to test his understanding more competently as the focus is now on meaning and not process.

4. Analysis of reading—general outline

The basic principle of reading analysis is to look and see what the child is trying to do, what strategies he employs and what knowledge he possesses. The focus, of course, has to be on what he finds difficult, and this involves looking at errors, though not only errors. In this approach errors are viewed, in any case, as possible sources of information and not simply as signs of failure.

First steps
The primary data for the analysis comes from the words which cause any kind of difficulty. By this I mean that any significant pause, part-word sounding out or error should be recorded. From this data we may make a major division between words that are given immediately, but inaccurately, and those where the child is aware of difficulty, which is acknowledged by a pause. The latter may or may not be accompanied by external evidence of word analysis. Sometimes analysis may only be inferred by the production of the correct word at the end of the pause. The following is the initial classification which I have found most useful:

WORD DIFFICULTY

Guess:	Pause:
(a) Immediate response error	(a) Pause—no response
(b) (correct—not identifiable)	(b) Pause—incorrect response
	(c) Pause—correct response
	(d) Pause—sounding out—incorrect response
	(e) Pause—sounding out—correct response

The difference between the immediate and the delayed response is one of strategy. In the first instance, the reader feels confident enough in his linguistic and word information to hazard a guess at the likely word. This is most likely to happen with short, grammatical words rather than longer, more conceptual ones. The latter are both more complex visually and semantically and therefore require greater care in analysis. It is these words which are the more likely to cause the reader to pause, since he recognizes that

84

neither his language ability, nor his word knowledge give him enough certainty for an immediate guess. Personality comes into it as well, as some individuals are more ready to 'chance their arm' than others. Yet another factor is that we learn, through experience, that longer words are both more difficult and, in a sense, more important. These are the words which carry the most information and they should have our full attention, as it is unwise to treat them in cavalier fashion. A comparison between the words that are guessed and the words that are analysed gives valuable insights into the way the reading task is being approached.

Within the 'pause' category, it is possible to subdivide on the basis of apparent word 'attack', on sounding out letters and parts of words or on silent strategies. This gives some indication of word knowledge and what have, traditionally, been regarded as phonic and look–say abilities. When one examines the data it is not possible to make a hard and fast distinction between a word analogy technique (akin to look–say) and a sound blending one (phonic). Both use additional language help and both, in fact, appear to be different stages in the development of word knowledge, with audible blending as an initial stage. In support of this contention, I would point out that audible sound strategies are usually a sign of great difficulty in encountering new words. My own records show that a greater proportion of errors occur using this technique than when processing is entirely silent. Of course, much of the silent processing is likely to be an internalized form of part-word sound correspondences, but this only strengthens the case against the necessity for audible analysis.

Second steps

In the preceding part of the analysis the emphasis has been upon word identification and word knowledge, because we have been looking at the difficult words as if they were isolated. I now want to consider the reading problems in relation to the interaction between the reading material and the child's linguistic abilities. We can get a lot of further information from looking at each difficult word in context. Each is in a sentence, which is itself embedded in text, which may, in turn, have associated pictures. All of these are potential sources of information for the child.

Do these influences show? If we look at the context for the guessed, immediate responses, a number of points are very clear. The first is that most children are obviously using language strategies in guessing, because their errors are usually grammatically acceptable in terms of the sentence up to that point. Either the guessed word is the same 'part of speech' as the printed word or it is different, but syntactically acceptable. There are other textual and contextual influences which may be teased out, but this immediate sentence influence is the most obvious.

A second important point which emerges is that children vary considerably in the way they use the part of the sentence following the guessed word. It is this stretch which invariably signals the syntactic or semantic anomaly, if there is one. The way the reader handles this information is very instructive. One's analysis should note whether words are corrected or not, whether the reader is picking up linguistic information and reading for sense.

Another point which may be made concerns the distinction between what we may call 'primary' and 'secondary' errors. With 'primary' errors it is some aspect of the word itself which causes the difficulty, whereas 'secondary' errors stem from some difficulty with a previous word. There is also an overlap between the two, since a word may not be recognized because the general context is unfamiliar or difficult.

The secondary error is an attempt to make the rest of the sentence conform to the earlier, and incorrect, interpretation. Here is one actual example:

Written   As the earth orbits the sun, we see a...
Spoken   As the earth orbits (pause) the sun WILL see a...

Here intonation gives the clue to the trouble. The word 'orbits' has been pronounced correctly but its meaning is not known and it has been interpreted as if it is analogous to 'runs' and therefore the end of the first clause. The reader is, therefore, looking for an auxiliary verb viz. 'Will' between 'sun' and 'see'.

What has been written in the preceding paragraphs about guessed errors can also be applied to the other category of the analysed words, where incorrect responses are made occasionally. However, the influence of the post-error part of the sentence is less because the pause for analysis is often so long as to disrupt the sense of the sentence entirely. A much greater emphasis is put on word knowledge in relation to the preceding text and context. Depending on his linguistic knowledge the child may either be asking 'Does that word I have pronounced make sense in context?' or 'Does that word make sense at all?'

Third and fourth steps

It is possible to carry the analysis further to include both the reading material and the teacher's help (where appropriate). One can turn the preceding step round and ask whether the errors are not so much the result of limited abilities as of limited clues in the text and context. Where a new word of some complexity is introduced into a story, for instance, does the illustration help, does the preceding text aid its identification? Are some of the errors induced by misleading or ambiguous clues? Finally, is the material appropriate to the child's linguistic and general knowledge?

The fourth step is only possible where the recording is of the child reading to the teacher. Here one can note the strategy the teacher adopts in helping the child. Is the style too intrusive? Does the teacher pounce on errors before the child has had the opportunity to correct them for himself? What is being praised, what censured? Is reading being presented as a word-perfect exercise (patently it is not)? What self-image is the teacher helping to create for the child? This is an ideal opportunity to find out.

READING ANALYSIS SHEET

Steps 1 and 2:

Guesses				Pauses			
Written	Spoken	Corrected	Notes	Written	Audible Sound	Actual Response	Notes

Guessing strategies: (e.g. proportion of high information words, primary and secondary errors, corrections)

Pause strategies: (e.g. length and complexity of words analysed, word analysis tactics, word knowledge)

Overall strategy:

(Systematic word differences between 'guess' and 'pause' words)

Step 3: Analysis of reading material:

Step 4: Analysis of teacher help:

In concluding this section of the chapter, I must make it clear that what has been suggested is what I have found useful. Others may prefer alternative methods of analysis. What cannot be denied is that the benefit of tape recording comes from the freedom to pursue one's own methods and to abandon them, if necessary, without losing the original data.

5. Analysis of reading—some specific contrasts

The discussion of reading analysis would not be complete without some indication of the contrasting approaches to reading which different children exhibit. I have chosen part of the reading performance of two children (J.G. and R.W.) because they are both known to be intelligent, yet one has made fast reading progress and the other quite slow progress. At the time these children were recorded, both were reading material which was roughly comparable. J.G. was 6 years old and R.W. 10 years old.

First J.G.s performance on a page from 'The Little Wooden Horse' (Ginn—*Time for Reading*):

Once Mr. Tortoise had a smooth(smoth) shell. But now (no) he has a cracked (craw..) shell. This is the story of how Mr. Tortoise cracked his shell. Mr. Tortoise walked very slowly. But he walked (very) and walked all day long. So he walked a long way. All the animals knew him. The lion knew (no) him and called out, 'Good morning, Mr. Tortoise.' 'Good morning, Lion,' said the (Mr.) tortoise.

→ intonation group between pauses
( ) word difficulty and approximate sound

There are a number of features of interest. The first is the language flow as indicated by the intonation patterns. Reading here is a smooth activity, with phrases and clauses being united through the tone of voice. Language, again, plays a significant part in three out of the four guessed errors, which appear to be anticipations linked to the preceding text. What is apparent as well is that linguistic processing continues after the words are spoken, because two out of the three were corrected as soon as the errors became apparent. The third error, 'Mr.' for 'the', was left uncorrected as it did not alter the sense of the sentence.

By and large, the words guessed at were short and 'low' informa-

Guesses				Pauses			
Written	*Spoken*	*Corrected*	*Notes*	*Written*	*Audible Sound*	*Actual Response*	*Notes*
now	no	?	another intervening error	smooth	✓	smoth	Text and picture no help
ø	very	✓	anticipated form from previous sentence	cracked	✓	craw..	Text and picture no help
knew	no	✓	anticipated speech (knowed)				
the	Mr.	—	anticipated form from previous sentence				

tion words. The two words which were analysed were 6 and 7 letters long, respectively, and high information words. It is interesting to note that, in both, some audible phonic strategy was attempted unsuccessfully.

The second reader (R.W.) read a number of pages from 'Night' (MacDonald *Starters*):

It is time for me to go to bed. Soon it will be dark. Most people sleep at night. Many animals (adults) sleep at night too. Some people work at night. They sleep in the day time. This nurse (noise) works at night. This man is a nightwatchman (nightwatchman). He is looking after a factory (factory). He has not seen the robbers. This machine prints newspapers. Men (man) work the machine at night.

⟵⟶ intonation group between pauses

( ) word difficulty and approximate sound

Guesses				Pauses			
Written	*Spoken*	*Corrected*	*Notes*	*Written*	*Audible Sound*	*Actual Response*	*Notes*
animals	adults	—	doesn't fit context	night-watchman	—	night-watch-man	Good pictorial clue
nurse	noise	✓	corrected immediately	factory	—	factory	Good pictorial clue
men	man	✓	unlikely choice for start of sentence				

As the two pieces of reading are about the same length, one can see that the error/difficulty rate is not particularly different for the two readers. What distinguishes them is the way the problems are handled, particularly in relation to language.

For R.W. we find that full language abilities do not play such an active part in his processing. Taking intonation groups first, we see that this reader is chopping the text into smaller segments, so that the same sense of flow is not present. This means that a much greater reliance has been put on the visual aspect of word identification, to the detriment of language involvement. Language abilities are being used, small phrases are read, but they are less involved than they might be.

All the guesses, too, are adequate linguistically; they are all possible at that point in the text on grammatical grounds. Both 'man' and 'adults' are somewhat unlikely, however, and the latter does not make very much sense in context. 'Adults' was not corrected, showing little reading for sense was taking place. In fact, 'noise' and 'man' were both corrected immediately, but probably on a 'second-look' basis, which is typical of the hesitant, uncertain reader.

An interesting point is that the guessed words are not short grammatical ones, but longer information carrying words. The reader has gambled (and failed) on words that are important both for present understanding and future processing. A direct comparison, on a 'parts of speech' basis, makes this difference between the two readers a very telling one:

	J.G.		R.W.	
	GUESSED	PAUSE	GUESSED	PAUSE
Noun	0	5	5	12
Verb	3	5	7	3
Adjective	1	5	5	2
Others	16	2	5	2
	20	17	19	17

Total 37
(522 words in text)

Total 36
(317 words in text)

Nouns, verbs and adjectives are, of course, the high information words; J.G. guessed at 4, R.W. guessed at 14. On the other hand, J.G. was much more prepared to guess at low information words

(16 against 5) which is a sign of reading flow and confidence. This greater language involvement in the smoothness, speed and certainty of reading is conspicuously lacking in R.W. who would be considered a poor or remedial reader for his age.

9 Meaning, method and materials

'A deeper understanding of what is involved in reading, and in learning to read, is far more important for the reading teacher than any expectation of better and more efficacious instructional materials.'

F. Smith (54)

1. Introduction

In this last chapter I want to consider how teachers, or any other interested adult for that matter, can set about helping each child to read effectively. This is not a matter of advocating particular methods or materials, but of organization coupled to flexibility.

In fact, I cannot do better than quote Stephen Wiseman on this subject. In the introduction to a study of reading methods in different infant schools, he wrote:

'What distinguishes the successful from the unsuccessful schools seems quite simple—the existence among their teachers of clearly defined objectives, of a workmanlike approach to their task, of a systematic and planned series of exercises and activities, and of an eclecticism in amalgamating various methods and choosing—at appropriate times—the essential from each. "Good" teachers and "good" schools are those which know what they want to do, plan how they intend to do it, and structure the activities of the day and week accordingly, and monitor the progress of their teaching.' (61)

This last sentence of Wiseman's points to the probable reasons for Kohl's complaint about 'problem teachers and problem schools'. (37)

2. Meaning

The emphasis throughout this chapter is on establishing reading for meaning. Such an approach means deliberately engaging higher orders of processing information in the knowledge that these themselves will be developed in the process. These 'higher orders' are, of course, thought and language, particularly where they apply to text. In this section of the chapter we will consider how the teacher can foster reading for meaning through classroom activities.

It is frequently said that the best method of learning to read is to read. (54) It does beg the question, however, of what you mean by reading. As we have seen, there are many ways of undertaking the processing of print, not all of which one would want to grace with the title 'reading'. I think it would be clearer, and more precise, to say that the way to learn to read is by reading for meaning.

What I have suggested is that a teacher can make great use of a tape (or cassette) recorder, both for the analysis and for the furtherance of reading abilities. For ordinary classroom activities, I would suggest that the child be given the opportunity to tape record the reading on his own. Child and teacher can then sit down together and play back the recording, discussing points as they arise.

There are a number of advantages to using this approach. First, it encourages the child to develop independent reading habits. It may also show that the reading material is too hard and that the child's seeming competence earlier was because of teacher support during the reading. It is very easy to be misled on this point; many children seem to be improving when all they are doing, really, is leaning more heavily on the aid the teacher is giving. The fact that the teacher is not involved in the actual reading allows the child to develop his own strategies. Too often, the teacher, anxious to correct errors, curtails this development by pointing out mistakes as they occur, without giving the child the opportunity to do so. The child will soon learn that he does not need to bother about monitoring his own readings, as the teacher is doing it for him. Another point is that the child can stop to analyse words (by switching off the recording) without the inhibiting and, sometimes, intimidating presence of the teacher making matters more difficult.

Further advantages to the tape recording technique come from the ability to play back what has been read. This enables the child to act as an observer–listener and so bring meaningful analysis to bear. It also means that the child has gone over the same material twice within a short space of time.

Like all techniques there are also difficulties and disadvantages associated with implementing it. The first is the demand on equipment which a school would face if all their teachers adopted the tape recording approach. Really, however, the demand ought to be periodic and mainly confined to the more junior classes. While there is considerable advantage to using a tape recorder in reading, it does involve reading out loud and this reduces the amount of silent reading the child undertakes. For this reason the teacher has got to keep an eye on the length of time a child is using this technique. As soon as is practicable, a switch should be made to a silent reading approach. Only where a child continues to have considerable difficulty with reading should the technique be used over a prolonged period of time.

Even if the teacher has no tape recorder to use, it is still possible to take advantage of some insights that recording reading has given. For instance, I think that it is of benefit, to both concerned, if the teacher simply acts as an uninvolved spectator when the child reads. As far as possible, the teacher should leave the child free to work out methods of tackling his own problems. This means, for the teacher, sitting and recording difficulties and learning strategies, but avoiding involvement unless it is absolutely necessary. It is far better to teach the reading skills independently than to disrupt the flow of reading, whatever it is, for on-the-spot tuition. In other words, the teacher's purpose in hearing a child read must be to get information to help in the planning of future meaningful activities.

3. Method

The teacher's role in reading development is to give help and then get out of the child's way as soon as possible. The sooner a child takes over its own organization of reading, the better. To do this the child must be able to undertake the same activities that the 'good' teacher does. (43) He must be able to define his goals in terms of his own information and reading needs. He must be able to select suitable sources of material to satisfy those needs. He must be able to extract the meaning from the materials and, in doing so, direct his own learning processes. Finally, he must be able to evaluate what he has read and learned and act accordingly. The teacher's job, in essence, is to make the child as self-supportive as possible. We do them no favours by teaching them dependence on our own methods and materials.

Of course, the teacher must provide support and guidance until the child is able to take the responsibility for the conduct of his own reading progress. This is a delicate task which involves setting general goals, but without dictatorial handling and undue restriction. The teacher must be aware of what reading is about and the many ways that competence may be achieved. Merritt (43) has complained that our conception of reading is often very narrow. We tend to think of it as the means of concentrated study, forgetting that skimming and scanning, for instance, are important methods of collecting information. If the teacher can bear the future needs of the child in mind, then the problems of providing appropriate reading experience are somewhat reduced. But if the most efficient use is to be made of the child's time in reading activities then it is necessary to plan accordingly.

In fact, there are a number of general considerations drawn from what has been written previously:

1. Start from where the child is. This means, in practice, undertaking an assessment in order to plan activities which will help groups of children in conjunction. We will consider more specific help later in the chapter.

2. Involve language and thought in all tasks. If a child does not, or cannot, use his abilities and knowledge in reading activities, then it is essential to show him how this can be achieved. One way to start is by getting the child to approach all tasks as problem-solving activities in which reasoned strategies will aid their solution. In particular, the advantages of deliberately using language to supplement other reading processes must be demonstrated.

3. Present material in such a way that it can be learned easily. There are a number of different considerations to be taken into account here.

   (a) Introduce new material in small amounts, otherwise processing restrictions will not enable the individual to cope with the onrush of information. Too great a proportion of new words in a story makes it very hard to understand, for instance.

   (b) An overall limitation on what is to be learned is a great

95

advantage, because it provides the conditions for the employment of strategies in learning. The realization that reading involves the use of a limited number of alphabet letters enables the child to start sorting out the important differences. The same applies to reading schemes which limit the vocabulary.

One occasionally comes across older children in remedial classes upon whom the motivational advantages of such systems are lost. Although they know they can improve and would like to read, the enormity of learning vast numbers of new words demoralizes them and they do not try. They just do not realize there are short cuts and that what one learns is an aid to further learning.

(c) Provide repetition without boring the children. I am not talking here simply of word repetition, but rather of text. The child, the second time through a story, will get more words right because he has absorbed much of the meaning. Repetition provides the child with opportunities to employ learning strategies which result in progressive mastery of text. We see this very clearly in young children who insist on our reading them the same story night after night because they have become so familiar with its meaning.

(d) Make the material as meaningful as possible so that higher orders of learning are engendered through the interaction between the material and the child's processing. Such a condition is the complement to 2 above, since it requires the active involvement of linguistic and intellectual abilities.

It is always fairly easy to establish learning through repetition. The typical sounds of alphabet letters are often taught this way, by presenting the letter and giving its sound. But if the letters are taught in isolation like this, it handicaps those children who have difficulty with categorizing the letters on their important distinguishing features. They tend to get in a hopeless muddle over similar-looking letters such as 'b' and 'd', for instance, because they have not focused on the different left-right orientation of the two letters.

One can reduce these problems from the outset by feeding the children's categorizing processes. This means presenting the letters together in a meaningful context so that the child can work on sorting out their distinctive features. Remedial teachers employ this technique when they use the word 'bed' to teach the letters 'b' and 'd'. What is hard is not associating letter with sound, but of distinguishing letter from letter.

4. Limit the child's dependence on the teacher. This is a most difficult area of a teacher's responsibilities towards a child because personality and social factors may be pushing the teacher in the opposite direction. Class differences are likely to play a major part from the outset. It is apparent, to anybody who stands outside an infants school at the end of the day, that concern over the child's introduction to reading is not the prerogative of just one class. It often forms the initial subject of conversation between mother and child whatever their social origins. But there are differences in attitude which are apparent from the questions they ask. The middle-class mother is likely to ask 'Did you read today?', whereas the working-class mother will probably say 'Has the teacher heard you read?' This difference in emphasis is probably correlated with attitudes towards the learning of skills. (7) The middle-class parents expect children to develop these skills through the child's own efforts, whereas the working-class parent places greater emphasis on the passing on of skills by verbal teaching. Working-class parents may become very irate when their children bring home books to read, because they see this as teachers shirking their responsibilities. I know of one teacher who, in these circumstances, was told in no uncertain terms where her duties lay. Such attitudes are likely to be absorbed by the children in that they expect to be taught how to read. They may not see themselves as active learners, and they may not see any reason why they should be so.

There are also certain personalities who like to depend on the teacher for all instruction. It is very difficult to get such children to undertake independent action. We do not help this type of child by giving him activities which are very much teacher dependent. It is my impression that far too much reading instruction, especially in remedial groups, is of this nature. Reading out loud is the prime example of an activity which we all make children carry on with too long. It carries the additional danger, found occasionally in poor readers, that the reading performance itself becomes all important as an audible sign of success.

5. Keep a continuous, but unobtrusive, check on reading progress. This applies as much to those children one considers are reading well as it does to those experiencing greater difficulty. It is better to make a large number of small changes in reading over

97

a period of time than to make a smaller number of radical ones at infrequent intervals. For the better reader, the teacher's interest should focus on how the child is undertaking the exploration of different areas of knowledge and how extensive is his interest in all forms of literature. For the poorer reader, reading progress must be interpreted more as an improved approach to reading, though the other considerations are no less important here as well.

If we now turn to more specific difficulties which a reading analysis may throw up, we find at least seven important general categories to look at: perception, memory, language abilities, intellectual abilities, personality, general knowledge and strategies.

PERCEPTION: On the visual side, one looks to see how many letters can be identified and what confusions occur. This gives some idea of how categorizing is proceeding. Similarly, the list of reading errors will provide evidence of difficulties above the individual letter level. However, it is unwise, in my opinion, to treat the above difficulties as if they occur in isolation and are purely perceptual. Both from the point of view of categorizing the mistakes and in helping the problems, it is better to put the mistakes or omissions in context. One looks to see the circumstances in which they were produced and the circumstances in which, one feels, they may be avoided. The confusion between 'b' and 'd', mentioned earlier in the chapter, is a good example of a common difficulty which may be avoided through the judicious use of meaningful material.

There may also be problems associated with auditory perception and the categorization of speech sounds, especially similar ones like /b/ and /p/ or /f/ and /v/ and /θ/. Unless these are distinguished consistently it is very difficult to link them with the appropriate visual configurations. Training should consist of presenting the confused sounds together within a meaningful context. For instance, one could ask a child to distinguish between 'bat' and 'pat' by requiring him to carry out an appropriate action on demand e.g. 'Give me a (bat/pat)'. It is possible to circumvent many of these difficulties by appealing to meaning and linguistic knowledge. The same goes for phonic difficulties where one looks to word knowledge and vocabulary for help.

MEMORY: A frequent complaint about the poor reader is that he does not retain what he has learned for very long, despite constant repetition. This condition is also associated with a word-by-word reading technique, which ignores language constraints. The problem, in both cases, is with meaning as much as memory. What is retained is a function of what is taken in, and this, in the case of the poor reader, is largely visual information. The perceptual act is not aided by meaningful linguistic constraints and, therefore, the child does not relate what he is seeing with established organization. Since this kind of link is vital to recall, the child is no better off the next time he comes across the same word. The problem for the teacher is to break this vicious circle by using material and illustration, so that the child will become aware of, and use, linguistic help. It is also useful to give the child training in memory strategies generally.

LANGUAGE ABILITIES: Much of what has already been written indicates that, by not employing linguistic knowledge, other problems are harder to solve. Reading for meaning involves a whole range of language activities which may be employed, from anticipatory guessing to the detailed analysis of textual meaning. These must be developed and used in order to read effectively. One should examine reading errors for lack of textual knowledge so that the right kind of background information may be introduced. One must be alert to the child who is struggling to summon up linguistic knowledge, but unsuccessfully. In reading a story about stolen money a boy reads, 'His father was glad to get the CRASH back.' He stops, obviously aware of what word is making nonsense of the sentence, but unable to resolve his dilemma. Subsequent questioning reveals he does know the word 'cash' and what it means. Here is a problem of linguistic 'flexibility' since most readers would have adjusted 'crash' to 'cash' with barely a second thought. Greater word knowledge and textual experience is the ultimate answer, but activities using the transformation of words may be a useful adjunct to reading.

INTELLECTUAL ABILITIES: The extent to which the child is using verbal reasoning, for instance, is an important factor in reading progress. This is linked inevitably with reading strategies. Does the child reason from picture to text in obtaining information about a word? Does the child reason out a rough meaning for a word that he cannot read? Is he making use of the implications which are signalled by the juxtaposition of pieces of information or through particular uses of language? These points, and others, are worth pursuing because it is possible to help the child obtain information much more efficiently in reading.

99

PERSONALITY: There are all sorts of additional problems which may be attributed to personality differences and styles of working. A child who is depressed and unhappy will not be very involved in working out the difficulties he encounters. In an investigation which I conducted, it was the more cheerful extroverted child who benefited more, in the long term, from reading help than the quieter withdrawn introvert.

Certain consistent behaviours make reading progress difficult. The extremes of haste and slowness are not helpful, the former because there is lack of consideration for meaning and the latter because meaning is lost through overlong deliberation. Other difficulties may show themselves as well. Children vary in their tolerance of their own mistakes; some are quite happy to 'plough on' making mistake after mistake, whereas others react strongly to the smallest of their own errors.

GENERAL KNOWLEDGE: While reading may be one of the principal methods of enlarging one's conceptions and experience about the world, the reverse is that lack of relevant knowledge is a serious handicap in reading itself. It is quite possible, as well, for a child to be able to read a word without understanding what it means. I gave an example earlier of a boy who read 'orbits' without knowing its meaning. It is up to the teacher to spot particular areas of weakness and to try to provide the relevant experience. A preliminary discussion of the child's book is often a very good way to introduce ideas and vocabulary for help in the short term.

STRATEGIES: Strategies are a deliberate attempt (though not necessarily formulated as such) to make use of the individual's abilities and knowledge. The more important of them were discussed in the previous chapter on reading analysis and will not be elaborated here. What the teacher must look for are inappropriate strategies, such as compulsive guessing and the compulsive sounding out of letters (luh–i–guh–huh–tuh as an attempt at 'light'). These may be remedied by showing the child how other tactics bring better chances of success. The analysis of strategies helps to pinpoint a child's particular weaknesses. One example, given before, was of a child who knew that the word 'crash' was wrong but could not rectify it. In cases like this the teacher must plan for both short-term and long-term objectives, which will help the child to have appropriate information available for use in his learning strategies.

4. Materials

There are two contrasting attitudes towards matching child and reading material. These may be characterized as: 1. Waiting for the child to fit the book, and 2. Fitting the book to the child. The former emphasizes 'reading readiness' and the latter individual motivation. Most teachers adopt a mixed method because limited time and resources do not allow them to adopt one approach exclusively.

Many reading schemes have pre-reading activities and materials designed to develop reading readiness and get the child off to a good start. They all purport, too, to be fitted to the child's needs in that they approach reading in easy stages. Motivation is engendered, not so much by the story content, as by the success which the structuring guarantees for the majority of children. The degree of advantage that the teacher gains in sticking to one scheme depends on the skill with which it has been put together and how it fits the children who use it. The teacher also knows what all the children have been reading in the previous class simply by noting which books they are currently reading. The disadvantages are the danger of boredom from the stilted language used and the expectation that the scheme will suit all the children.

Trying to find books which suit different individuals is a much more difficult and arduous task for the teacher. However, it is one alternative for those children who do not get on with the reading scheme. In many cases this can be done by simply switching to an alternative scheme, if this is available.

But the search for books to fit the individual need not be a tactic of desperation. Many people are keenly aware of the limitations which reading schemes impose on the development of all readers, but especially the better ones. Under this kind of pressure children's book publishers are currently producing vast numbers of simple factual reading books with plenty of supportive illustration. There is plenty of scope here to motivate all children, including those who are reluctant to start reading. Other series have been produced which do try to match the children's own language and circumstances. They offer greater interest to some children than many of the traditional schemes.

With all this choice it should not be beyond most teachers to help children to follow interests, to start them reading widely and to provide reading experience which they lack. This is the task the teacher should be following, anyway, for the good reader who has gone beyond the reading scheme.

For the beginner reader there are many other alternatives which may be explored in the attempt to get them started on processing print. One such is to use a child's own stories, written in his own language style. This is the approach which the authors of *Breakthrough to Literacy* recommend as part of the use of their material (41). The more daring and ambitious teachers may think of extending this idea by producing their own books for the children to read. What could be more motivating than having a book written specially for you?

We have not yet exhausted the possibilities of involving children in processing print. There are, as Herbert Kohl has pointed out, (37) innumerable objects in a child's environment for him to read, such as bus-stop signs, street names, signposts, cereal packets, jam-jar labels, television adverts, comics, newspaper headlines and so forth. While the opportunity to make use of these lies largely with the parents, the teacher may find it very helpful to bring examples into the classroom for activities and topics there. Many parents comment that they have become aware of their child's awakening interest in print because the child has suddenly started to read these environmental forms of print.

As far as preparing the child for reading is concerned, there are many materials and activities which a teacher may employ. In fact, there are almost limitless ways to build up basic textual abilities. It is preferable, however, to use materials which link up with reading either thematically or by encouraging the child to develop appropriate reading habits. There are a number of schemes on the market which are designed to encourage language and thinking activities. I shall describe my own briefly (27). It was designed to supplement the approach to reading discussed in this book and it grew out of work with children who have special learning difficulties.

I was concerned to suggest activities which would develop the children's experience of creating text, while also helping other processes such as memory, concept formation and strategies. These objectives are only obtained through the active participation of the teacher in developing the use of the picture material that the scheme consists of. It is essential, therefore, that the teacher should know what he or she wants, in terms of objectives. I incorporated the teacher into the scheme deliberately by leaving the detailed planning of sequences for the teachers to fit into their own particular circumstances.

The scheme consists of three sets of picture cards which are con-cerned with language and conceptual thinking, language and stories, and language and situation. The first set of cards consists of paired cut-up sheets of pictures, with a theme per pair of sheets e.g. items of food and drink, clothing, occupations. These are designed for active concept exploration using sorting tasks and group discussions. The sheets are paired so that the traditional type of memory game using cards can be played. In addition, by using an assorted pile of cards, the teacher can get the children exploring and expanding their own textual abilities. This is done by picking out at random two cards, say, and asking for a sensible statement which includes the names of both items on the cards. By varying the number of cards used, this task can be made as simple or hard as the teacher requires.

The other two sets of cards allow the teacher to use activities which involve language-for-description and language-for-stories. The former consists of illustrations of familiar situations such as 'shopping in the high street' and 'playing in the park'. From this material, descriptive-memory activities are developed. The lan-guage-for-stories material is a number of different picture stories illustrating sequences of actions associated with the scenes of the previous card set. Again, a variety of language activities can be developed at any level the teacher feels appropriate.

What is particularly important is that, in each activity, the emphasis is upon the way the children want to respond to the pictures. There is no question of right or wrong, simply of which way a child has chosen to represent what he has seen or remembered. Progress comes through active involvement, through listening to the way other children represent themselves linguistically, and through discussion of the pros and cons of par-ticular contributions.

There are two further important points to be made: the first is that, by improving a child's ability to respond linguistically to pictorial representation, one is not automatically improving read-ing abilities. This is another task for the teacher: to ensure that what is learned or developed in one context is applied in another. The second point has a very general application. In producing situations where the child's response is always acceptable, one is creating a good image for the child. This is specially important for most of the poorer readers, who have a correspondingly poor image of themselves. It is essential that a child thinks of himself as a learner before one can hope to get him to approach reading in this manner.

5. **Coda**

We have come full circle; that is, back to a consideration of what the child gets from the educational situation in which he is placed. In the initial chapters of this book I introduced the idea that the remedial and compensatory programmes were based on blaming the child, albeit implicitly, for being a failure, for not conforming to the expectations that society has for us all. We saw that this diverted attention from a consideration of the child as learner and from the school's part in educating that child.

I suggested that a more positive approach was needed, one which would help the child to develop naturally from what he was already doing. As language is central to all educational processes, and is crucially involved in reading, it was sensible for teachers to know more about it. The development of a child's textual abilities was then elaborated, together with the way children handle reading development. This led to a consideration of good and poor readers, the strategies they employ, and the way a teacher may assess what is happening.

Finally, I undertook a brief exploration of what could be done through language involvement to supply the children with a positive learning environment in which they could master the problems of literacy, using their own talents and abilities. In a previous volume of this series, Geoffrey Thornton wrote: 'Despite a great deal of dedicated work going on in Remedial departments, there has so far been little serious attempt to evolve teaching techniques based upon sound linguistic principles.' (56) This is a charge laid against us all and it demands a reply from each one of us. I have outlined above my own response and some of the theory behind it. My hope is that I have convinced you, the reader, that a linguistic approach is not only feasible, but necessary.

In the final analysis, the kind of learning environment we supply for each child is of paramount importance. Let us make sure that it is a positive one, one in which a child feels free to make progress in making sense of the world through his own efforts.

Bibliography

1. Bateman, B. (1965) 'An educator's view of a diagnostic approach to learning disorders' in *Learning Disorders*, Volume 1 (Seattle seguin School).
2. Baratz, S. S., Baratz, J. C. (1969) 'Negro Ghetto Children and Urban Education: A Cultural Solution'. Social Education 33.
3. Beard, R. M. (1969) *An Outline of Piaget's Developmental Psychology* (RKP).
4. Beez, W. V. (1968) 'Influence of biased psychological reports on teacher behaviour and pupil performance'. Proceedings 76th Annual Convention of American Psychological Association.
5. Bernstein, B. (1961) 'Social Structure, Language and Learning'. Educational Research 3. 163–76.
6. Bernstein, B. (1973) *Class, Codes and Control* Vol. 1 (Paladin).
7. Bernstein, B., Henderson, D. (1973) 'Social class differences in the relevance of language to socialization' in B. Bernstein (ed.) *Class, Codes and Control* Volume 2 (R.K.P.).
8. Bever, T. G. (1970) 'The cognitive basis for linguistic structures' in J. R. Hayes (ed.) *Cognition and the Development of Language* (Wiley).
9. Bloomfield, L. (1942) 'Linguistics and Reading'. Elementary English 19.
10. Britton, J. (1970) *Language and Learning* (Pelican).
11. Bruner, J. S. (1957) 'On Perceptual Readiness'. Psychological Review 64. 123–152.
12. Cashdan, A. (1970) 'Backward readers—research on auditory visual integration' in W. K. Gardner (ed.) *Reading Skills: Theory and Practice* (Ward Lock Educational).
13. Cattell, J. McK. (1947) *James McKeen Cattell, Man of Science. 1860–1944* (Science Press).
14. Chalfant, J. C., Scheffelin, M. A. (1969) *Central Processing Dysfunctions in Children* (U.S. Dept. of Health, Education and Welfare).
15. Clay, M. M. (1969) 'Reading errors and self-correction behaviour'. Brit.J.Educ.Psychol. 39. 47.

16. Cruickshank, W. (1974) Lecture: 'Specific Learning Difficulties'. Birmingham University.
17. Deutsch, M. et al. (1967) *The disadvantaged child* (Basic Books).
18. Douglas, J. W. B. (1966) *The Home and the School* (MacGibbon & Kee).
19. Eisenberg, L. (1966) 'The epidemiology of reading retardation and a program for preventive intervention' in J. Money (ed.) *The Disabled Reader* (Johns Hopkins Press).
20. Flanagan, J. L. (1965) *Speech Analysis, Synthesis and Perception* (Basic Books).
21. Flavell J. H. (1970) 'Developmental studies of mediated memory' in L. Lipsitt, H. Reese (eds.) *Advances in Child Development and Behaviour* (Academic Press).
22. Fry, D. B. (1970) 'Speech reception and perception' in J. Lyons (ed.) *New Horizons in Linguistics* (Pelican).
23. Fuchs, E. (1968) 'How teachers learn to help children fail'. Transactions 45–9.
24. Gibson, E. J. (1965) 'Learning to Read'. Science. 148. 1066–72.
25. Gibson, E. J. (1970) 'The Ontogeny of Reading'. American Psychologist. 25. 2. 136–43.
26. Goodman, K. S. (1969) 'Analysis of Oral Reading Miscues: Applied Psycholinguistics'. Reading Research Quarterly. 5. 1. 9–30.
27. Gurney, R. S. (1975) *Play and Say* (Edward Arnold).
28. Hagen, J. W. (1972) 'Strategies for Remembering' in S. Farnham-Diggory (ed.) *Information Processing in Children* (Academic Press).
29. Halliday, M. A. K. (1973) Introduction to *Class, Codes and Control* (Vol. II), B. Bernstein (RKP).
30. Halliday, M. A. K. and Ruqaiya Hasan (1976) *Cohesion in English* (Longman).
31. Halliday, M. A. K. (1975) *Learning how to mean* (Edward Arnold).
32. Halliday, M. A. K., McKintosh, A., Strevens, P. (1964) *The Linguistic Sciences and Language Teaching* (Longman).
33. Hirsch, K. De et al. (1967) *Predicting Reading Failure. A preliminary study* (Harper).
34. Holmes, D. L. (1971) 'The Independence of Letter, Word, and Meaning Identification in Reading'. Reading Research Quarterly. 6. 3. 394–415.
35. Horner, V. M., Gussow, J. D. (1972) 'John and Mary: A Pilot Study in Linguistic Ecology' in C. B. Cazden et al. (eds.) *Functions of Language in the Classroom* (Teachers College Press).
36. Kass, C. (1966) Conference on Learning Disabilities. Lawrence, Kansas.
37. Kohl, H. (1973) *Reading, How to* (Penguin).
38. Kolers, P. A. (1973) 'Three Stages in Reading' in F. Smith (ed.) *Psycholinguistics and Reading* (Holt, Rinehart and Winston).
39. Lenneberg, E. H. (1967) *The biological foundations of language* (Wiley).

40. Liberman, A. M. et al. (1957) 'The discrimination of speech sounds within and across phoneme boundaries'. J.E.Psch. 54. 358–68.
41. Mackay, D., Thompson, B., Schaub, P. (1970) *Breakthrough to Literacy* (Longman).
42. Meredith, P. (1974) 'A Century of Regression'. Forum vol. 16, no. 2.
43. Merritt, J. (1974) Lecture on 'Reading and the Curriculum'. Birmingham University.
44. Miller, G. (1970) 'The magical number seven, plus or minus two: some limits on our capacity for processing information'. in *The Psychology of Communication* (Pelican).
45. Neale, M. D. (1966) *Neale Analysis of Reading Abilities* (MacMillan).
46. Neisser, U. (1967) *Cognitive Psychology* (Appleton-Century-Crofts).
47. Nelson, K. (1973) *Structure and Strategy in Learning to talk.* (Univ. of Chicago Press).
48. Newsom, J. H. (1963) *Half our Future* (HMSO).
49. Piaget, J. (1954) *The construction of reality in the child* (Basic Books).
50. Piaget, J. (1971) *Structuralism* (RKP).
51. Piaget, J., Inhelder, B. (1969) *The Psychology of the Child* (RKP).
52. Ruddell, R. B. (1967) 'Reading instruction in first grade with varying emphasis on the regularity of grapheme-phoneme correspondences and the relation of language structure to meaning—extended into second grade.' Reading Teacher. 20. 730–739.
53. Slobin, D. I. (1972) 'Seven Questions about Language Development' in P. C. Dodwell (ed.) *New Horizons in Psychology 2* (Penguin).
54. Smith, F. (1973) *Psycholinguistics and Reading* (Holt, Rinehart and Winston).
55. Strickland, R. (1962) *The Language of elementary school children: its relationship to the language of reading textbooks and the quality of reading of selected children* (Univ. of Indiana Press).
56. Thornton, G. M. (1974) *Language, Experience and School* (Edward Arnold).
57. Turner, G. W. (1973) *Stylistics* (Pelican).
58. Vernon, M. D. (1971) *Reading and its Difficulties* (Cambridge Univ. Press).
59. Vigotsky, L. S. (1934) *Thought and language* (English tr., MIT Press).
60. Wiseman, S. (1967) The Manchester Survey in Plowden Report, Volume 2 (HMSO).
61. Wiseman, S. (1971) Preface to *The Roots of Reading* by Cane, B., Smithers, J. (NFER).
62. Worthington, A. G., Dixon, N. F. (1964) 'Changes in guessing habits as a function of subliminal stimulation'. Acta Psychol. 22. 338–347.

Further reading

Ashworth, E. *Language in the Junior School* (Edward Arnold, 1973).
Britton, J. *Language and Learning* (Penguin, 1970).
Cazden, C. B., et al. (eds.) *Functions of Language in the Classroom* (Teachers College Press, 1972).
Creber, J. W. P. *Lost for Words* (Penguin, 1972).
Halliday, M. A. K. *Explorations in the Functions of Language* (Edward Arnold, 1973).
Halliday, M. A. K. *Learning How to Mean* (Edward Arnold, 1975).
Keddie, N. (ed.) *tinker, tailor... The Myth of Cultural Deprivation* (Penguin, 1973).
Kohl, H. *Reading, How to* (Penguin, 1974).
McCullagh, S. *Into New Worlds* (Hart Davis Educational, 1974).
Moyle, D. *The Teaching of Reading* (Ward Lock, 1968).
Reid, J. F. (ed.) *Reading: Problems and Practices* (Ward Lock, 1972).
Rosen, C., Rosen, H. *The Language of Primary School Children* (Penguin, 1973).
Smith, F. *Psycholinguistics and Reading* (Holt, Rinehart and Winston, 1973).
Thornton, G. M. *Language, Experience and School* (Edward Arnold, 1974).
Vernon, M. D. *Reading and its Difficulties* (Cambridge Univ. Press).